QUICK GUIDE TO CUBAN SPANISH

JARED ROMEY

SPEAKING LATINO KUDOS

"Jared is the go-to guy for anyone learning or considering learning Spanish, and he'll blow you away with how much he knows about the Latin American varieties of the language."

- Donovan Nagel, Mezzofanti Guild: An Online Community of Serious Language Learners

"Romey translates common colloquialisms into English so that Americans can actually understand what the heck locals are saying when they visit South American countries."

- Monica Garske, AOL News

"Acabo de descubrir Speakinglatino.com. Que sitio más padre, chido, chévere, tuanis, bacán..."

- Jake Fisher comment on Facebook

"@JaredRomey ¡¡¡Me ca*** de risa!!! ¡Buenísimo! I had to pause several times to recover from laughing! You made my day!"

- @MultiMae from Mae's Language Lounge Blog via Twitter

TABLE OF CONTENTS

Useful external links

ABOUT THE
"QUICK GUIDE TO CUBAN SPANISH"

Perhaps you are Cuban, your family is from Cuba or you have Cuban friends. Maybe this Caribbean island is a faraway dream destination for you. Or maybe you are American and are prohibited by your government to visit. No matter what the reasons, many people are curious about issues related to Cuba and one of the fun topics people explore is its rich slang.

With the help of native Cubans we compiled this collection of words and phrases used on the largest island of the Antilles. We concisely explain them in English and share example sentences.

In this book you will find Spanish words that have a particular meaning or use for Cubans. You'll find some examples of words that are used regionally and the vulgar words that are inevitable in colloquial Spanish.

The Quick Guide to Cuban Spanish includes a total of 952 words, phrases or sayings

that have been used for generations. In addition the words are paired with 429 synonyms or related words and 430 entries include at least one example sentence.

Each entry is presented as follows:

> **empingao:** 1) excellent quality 2) annoyed, mad
> SYN: 1) buenísimo, entoletao 2) berreao, encabronao, encojonao, volao
> ANT: 1) pésimo, de mala calidad
> ✐ *1) El carro nuevo que me compré está empingao. 2) Estoy empingao contigo.*

Abbreviations and Symbols:
SYN: synonyms, similar or related words
ANT: antonyms
✐ example sentence

I would like to especially thank Taimí Antigua Lorenzo and Tania García for helping in the process of publishing this book.

Finally, I invite you to share with me your experiences related to Cuban Spanish. If you have anecdotes, questions, additions or corrections that can improve this project, write me at: jared@speakinglatino.com

SPANISH WORDS & PHRASES FROM CUBA

A

¿a santo de qué?: an expression of protest or disagreement
SYN: ¿Y por qué?
✐ *¿A santo de qué tengo que pagar doble?*

a la bartola: on the fly, careless
SYN: al retortero

a la bola: to be naked
SYN: desnudo, en pelota
ANT: vestido
✐ *Entré al cuarto y ella estaba a la bola.*

a la cubana: any food dish made with tomato pureé and whatever is on hand
✐ *Ayer cociné un arroz imperial a la cubana.*

a mi me gusta el café claro y el chocolate espeso: phrase that means someone likes the things well done; being clear and transparent with others
SYN: cuentas claras conservan amistades

a tres por kilo: 1) in abundance 2) refers to something of poor quality
✐ *1) Están a tres por kilo donde quiera.*
2) Por andar con mujeres de a tres por kilo me perdí lo mejor de mi vida.

absorbente: a drinking straw
✐ *Dale un absorbente para que no se ensucie.*

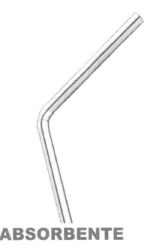

ABSORBENTE

acabar con la quinta y con los mangos: to completely destroy everything
SYN: acabar con malanga y su puesto de viandas

acabar como la fiesta del Guatao: to get off to a good start and all of a sudden everything goes downhill and ends badly
✐ *Aquello se acabó mal, como la fiesta del Guatao.*

achantado: a mix of lazy and comfortable
SYN: acomodado
ANT: trabajador
✐ *Estás ahí achantado sin hacer nada.*

aché: a word from the *Santería* religion that means good things, luck
SYN: don de virtud
ANT: obsorbo, estar obsorbo
✐ *Esa señora tiene tremendo aché.*

acojonante: bothersome, scary, impressive
SYN: que da miedo
✐ *La película estaba acojonante.*

acojonarse: to be scared
SYN: asustado, apencarse, apendejarse, arratonarse
ANT: sin temor
✐ *Cuando vio al león se quedó acojonado.*

ACOJONARSE

acoquinado: frightened
SYN: acobardado
✐ *Está acoquinado del miedo.*

acotejar: arrange,

9

sort, place items neatly in a given space, to organize
SYN: arreglar

adelantao or **adelantá:** a mulatto with more white features than black features

adré or **adresmente:** from the word in Spanish *adrede*, on purpose, intentionally

afeitar: to kill, murder
SYN: chapear, guisar, ñampiar

agarrado: to not like to share, stingy
SYN: tacaño
ANT: generoso
✐ *Es tremendo agarrado, no quería soltar ni un peso.*

agarrar con las manos en la masa: to get caught doing something wrong
SYN: ¡Lo cogieron asando maíz!

aguacate: a young man that is doing obligatory military service, the name comes from the avocado colored uniform

aguaje: braggart, boastful
SYN: fanfarrón, guapería, alarde
ANT: modesto, humilde
✐ *Yo hablo con aguaje porque soy así, si no te gusta fájate.*

aguajirarse: not confident, timid or shy

aguantar paquetes: to put up with someone's bad behavior
SYN: aguantar zoqueterías
✐ *Ya no te voy a aguantar más paquetes.*

aguantatarros: a person who tolerates

or is aware of the infidelity of their partner
SYN: aguantón

aguantón: a person who tolerates the infidelity of their partner
SYN: aguantatarros

ahorita or **horita:** in a while
✎ *Ahorita me voy a bañar.*

ají: a pepper, in many forms: small, big, spicy or non spicy, red, green, yellow.
✎ *Échale ají para que sepa rico.*

AJÍ

ajiaco: 1) confusion, disorder 2) a stew 3) complicated, intricate situation

ajumarse: to get drunk

SYN: emborracharse, juma, curdo / curda, estar curda, ponerse, nota, jalao, ponerse como una cuba

ajustador: a bra

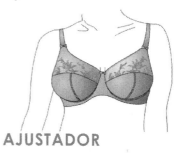

AJUSTADOR

al duro y sin guante: 1) to the point 2) rigorous, ruthlessly
✎ *La contraloría está trabajando al duro y sin guante.*

al retortero: careless, with no order
SYN: a la bartola
✎ *Ella anda al retortero por todo el barrio.*

¡alabao!: expression of admiration and exclamation, similar to OMG in English
SYN: ¡coño!
✎ *¡Alabao! Mira*

11

lo que esta está diciendo ahora.

alarde: to show things off or brag to create envy in others
SYN: ostentación, jactancia
✐ Siempre se comporta con un alarde, como si él fuera el ombligo del mundo.

aletazo: a blow given with an open hand or fist
SYN: galúa, piñazo, trompón, fuetazo, avión, tanganazo, mameyazo, viandazo
✐ ¿La mujer le dio un aletazo?

alfiler de criandera: safety pin
SYN: imperdible

ALFILER DE CRIANDERA

almendrón: an old car, mostly with the shape of the first, second and third generations of the Chevrolet Bel Air, most often used as taxis
✐ Me vino a buscar en un almendrón.

amanerado: an effeminate man, not necessarily homosexual
SYN: afeminado, amujerado
✐ Yo lo noto un poco amanerado, míralo como habla.

amarrar: to set, to arrange or to agree something with another person

amarrarse: literally means "to tie yourself," to get married

ambia: friend
SYN: asere, consorte, ecobio, compay, monina, nagüe, socio, cúmbila, yunta, pata

✎ *Asere mi ambia.*

ambientoso: 1) bully, aggressive, quarrelsome 2) a vulgar behaving person
SYN: 1) guapo

amelcocharse: to be extremely in love with someone

AMELCOCHARSE

analfaburro: dumb, stupid
SYN: anormal, bruto, ñame, ñame con corbata, cayuco, analfacebolleta, seboruco, berraco, zocotroco, no tener dos dedos de frente
ANT: filtro, inteligente
✎ *¿Acere, todavía no entiendes? ¿Tú eres un poco analfaburro no?*

analfacebolleta or **analfacebollón:** see *analfaburro*

andancio: a seasonal cold or flu
✎ *Ese andancio provoca mucha fiebre.*

anoncillo: a regional word for *mamoncillo*

antiflogitínico: indifferent, irrelevant, innocuous
✎ *Lo que sea que me escribas me es totalmente antiflogitínico.*

apearse: 1) to eat with the hands, with no cutlery 2) to dismount from a horse, or get out of a vehicle
SYN: 2) bajarse de
ANT: 2) subirse a
✎ *2) Apéate del carro que hay que empujarlo.*

apencarse: to be afraid, scared

SYN: acojonarse, apedendejarse, arratonarse
ANT: envalentonarse
✎ *No te me apenques ahora.*

apendejarse: to be afraid or scared
SYN: acojonarse, apencarse, apedendejarse, arratonarse
✎ *Te apendejaste por el tipo ese.*

aplatanar or **aplatanado:** accustom oneself to, acclimatize
SYN: adaptado
ANT: inadaptado
✎ *Ya me siento aplatanado en este país.*

apretar: 1) to have sexual contact, but not penetration 2) to exaggerate too much
SYN: 1) agarrar
✎ *1) ¿Y ellos dos estaban apretando?*

aquí el que no tiene de congo, tiene de carabalí: phrase to mean that in Cuba most people have African ancestors

armar un titingó: to make trouble, even to the point of fighting
✎ *En el solar se armó tremendo titingó.*

armatroste: something old and ugly, such as furniture or a car
SYN: tareco
✎ *¡Qué feo, parece un armatroste!*

arrancao: see *estar arrancao*

arrascar: to scratch
✎ *Arráscame la espalda que no llego.*

arratonarse: to be afraid or scared
SYN: acojonarse, apencarse, apedendejarse

arroz con mango: disaster, mess, confusion
SYN: desbarajuste

aruñar: to struggle or fight for something
SYN: guapear
✐ *¡Aruña si lo quieres!*

asere or **acere:** dude, buddy, pal
SYN: consorte, ecobio, ambia, compay, monina, nagüe, socio, cúmbila, yunta, pata
ANT: enemigo
✐ *¡Coño, asere no me digas eso!*

atacante: extremely annoying
SYN: insoportable, impertinente
✐ *¡Asere estás atacante, no te soporto!*

atrincar: to press, to oppress

avión or **avioneta:** a hit, a punch
SYN: aletazo, galúa, piñazo, trompón, fuetazo, tanganazo, mameyazo, viandazo

ayaca: the Cuban tamale
SYN: tayuyo or tallullo (in certain areas of Cuba), hallaca, hayaca
✐ *Comimos un poco de ayaca anoche. ¡Qué ricoooo!*

azulejo: policemen, in blue uniforms
SYN: fiana, meta
✐ *¡Cuidado que hay un azulejo allí¡*

CHECK OUT THE SPEAKING LATINO ARTICLES ON <u>CUBA</u> & <u>CUBAN SPANISH</u>!

DON'T MISS THESE:

- THE MOST AUTHENTIC WORD IN CUBAN SPANISH: <u>ASERE</u>

- DECODING A CUBAN MENU: 14 CUBAN SPANISH <u>FOOD WORDS AND DISHES</u>

- INFOGRAPHIC: 13 RANDOM <u>FUN FACTS ABOUT CUBA</u>

🖱 http://goo.gl/Y7sdAE

B

babalao: the priest in the *Santería* religion

baboso: 1) a person who talks a lot without saying much, to the point of being annoying 2) a boyfriend or girlfriend who is always dependent on, hanging on his / her partner
SYN: pegajoso
✐ *Yo le digo que me deje tranquila pero entonces me llama de nuevo, es un baboso.*

bacán: a good, cool
✐ *Él es un bacán, siempre nos invita cada vez que nos encontramos.*

bachata: party, hubbub, noise, commotion
SYN: fandango
✐ *¿Y esta bachata? ¡Les dije que se pusieran a trabajar!*

bailar la suiza: jump rope

BAILAR LA SUIZA

bajablumer: homemade rum of poor quality, the literal translation is a "panty lowerer"
✐ *¡Ah, no! ¿De dónde sacaste el bajablumers este?*

bajareque: a tiny, fragile house made from straw, rubbish and pieces of wood
SYN: casucha
✐ *Ella vive en un pobre bajareque.*

bajichupa or **baja y chupa:** a tube top
✐ *¡Mírala con un bajichupa qué sexy!*

17

BALA

bala: 1) bullet 2) motorcycle 3) cigarette
SYN: 3) bate
✐ *3) ¡Estoy loco por fumarme una bala!*

balde: a bucket on the eastern part of Cuba
SYN: cubo

bañadera: bathtub
✐ *La bañadera no es lo mismo que la ducha.*

BAÑADERA

baracutey: a person living alone, with no company

barbacoa: the construction of an extra wall dividing a room into two bedrooms to save space
✐ *Tremenda barbacoa que hicieron aquí, el techo me roza la cabeza.*

bárbaro: valiant, courageous, brave
SYN: volao
ANT: cobarde
✐ *Tu hermano es un bárbaro en el dominó.*

barco: an irresponsible and unreliable person, not fulfill a promise
SYN: irresponsable
✐ *Eres tremendo barco, siempre llegas tarde.*

baro: 1) money 2) one peso
SYN: 1) guaniquiqui, caña, piticlinis, pesos, fulas, plata, pasta, chavito

✐ 1) Hoy cobré, me llegó el baro.

BARO

barretín: a difficult, annoying or complicated issue
SYN: podrida, tiñosa

batacazo: a very hard hit, most often with a solid object
SYN: toletazo, trancazo
✐ Se ha dado un batacazo en la cabeza.

bateo: problem, debate, turmoil, to argue
SYN: candanga
✐ El niño me dio un bateo terrible.

batido de plomo: see chorro de plomo

bayú: commotion, hubbub, disorder

SYN: bonche
✐ El bayú comenzó cuando la profesora dejó el aula.

bayusero: a person that likes to create a commotion or bayú

bemba: thick lips

BEMBA

bembos: lips of the vagina
✐ Lo hicieron tanto que le dejó los bembos rojos.

berracá or berracada: foolishness

berraco: dumb, stupid
SYN: bruto, analfaburro, ñame, ñame con corbata, cayuco, analfacebolleta,

19

seboruco, zocotroco, no tener dos dedos de frente

berreao or **berrearse:** mad, upset
SYN: encabronao, empingao, encojonao, volao
ANT: estar en talla
✎ *No me digas que ya estás berreao, si solo estamos jugando. / Asere no te berrees por esa bobería.*

berro: fury, anger
SYN: enfado
✎ *¡Cogí un clase de berro con mi hermano!*

bibijagua: large, red ants that stink
✎ *Ten cuidado que aquí hay bibijagüas.*

bicha: a slut
SYN: zorra, descarada
ANT: decente
✎ *Pareces tremenda bicha con esa ropa.*

bicho: penis

20

SYN: cabilla, mandao, morronga, morrongón, pinga, tolete

bici-taxi: long bicycles with more than two seats in the back, used by tourists as taxis
✎ *¿Perdone, sabe usted dónde puedo encontrar un bici-taxi?*

bilongo: witchcraft
✎ *No camines por allí que hay un bilongo.*

birula: bicycle
SYN: bicicleta, chivo
✎ *¿Me prestas tu birula para ir al mercado?*

BIRULA

bisne: illegal business, from the English "business"

✐ ¿Quieres hacer un bisne conmigo?

bisnear: to do business illegally
SYN: negociar
✐ ¿De qué están hablando ellos? Están bisneando.

bistec or **bisté:** 1) a steak 2) a type haircut that just covers one eye and is used by the Emos (urban tribe)
✐ 1) Me acabo de comer tremendo bisté.

bloqueado: someone that doesn't understand what was explained to him
SYN: botao
ANT: estar claro, tener abiertas las entendederas
✐ Está bloqueada cuando se habla de computación.

blúmer: women's panties
✐ Niña cuidado con el viento que se te ve el blúmer.

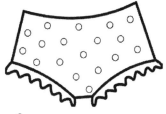

BLÚMER

bocadito: a small sandwich, typical for parties and birthdays
✐ Pasa los bocaditos, están riquísimos.

bocajarro or **boca e' jarro:** 1) a person that has a big mouth, who likes to brag 2) to say something directly, straight out
✐ 1) Oye tú, bocajarro, ven acá. 2) Le dio la mala noticia sin contemplaciones, a boca e' jarro.

bofe: annoying, undesirable
SYN: pesao, hígado, inmetible
✐ Eres un bofe, no te soporto.

bohío: a hut
✎ *Yo viví en un bohío de guano y tabla de palma.*

bola: news or rumors that travel on the street mostly without having a reliable source
✎ *No te imaginas la bola que te voy a contar.*

bollo: pussy
SYN: crica, papaya
✎ *No me sale del bollo. (This expression means "No me da la gana.")*

bollúa: the equivalent to man *cojonú* or *tener cojones* (to have balls) but for a woman: 1) big pussy 2) a bold woman 3) lazy woman
SYN: papayúa

bomba: the Cuban $20.00 bill
✎ *Sólo me queda una bomba en la billetera.*

bonche: 1) a party, celebration 2) can also mean joke, to make fun of someone
SYN: 1) guasanga 2) jarana
✎ *2) Le armamos tremendo bonche por los pantalones tan feos que llevaba puestos.*

boniatillo: 1) sweet made from boiled and sieved boniato, the pulp is mixed with sugar and cinnamon 2) an elusive person

BONIATO

boniato: white yam, sweet potato

bonitillo: a handsome man
SYN: estar bueno
ANT: feo
✎ *Abuelo estás bonitillo hoy.*

botarse pa'l solar (botarse para el solar): to behave rudely and aggressively
SYN: tirarse pa'l solar

botella: 1) hitchhiking 2) to have a job where the person receives a salary but does nothing useful
SYN: 2) empleo, pincha
✎ 1) ¿Me puede dar una botella hasta el Vedado? / Cogí botella hasta Santa Clara ? Llegue a mi casa gracias a que pedí botella. 2) Ese trabajo de ella no es más que una botella.

BOTELLA

botero: a private driver, not necessarily a taxi driver

✎ Llegué a tiempo gracias a un botero.

brete: a rumor that is most likely to end in something bad
SYN: titingó
✎ No formes más brete que lo único que haces es empeorar las cosas.

bretero: a gossip person
SYN: un lleva y trae, chismoso
✎ ¡No seas bretera!

bróder: anglicism from "brother" commonly used among men

buchipluma: braggart

buena hoja: a person that is good in bed

bugarrón: an insulting, offensive term for a homosexual that behaves like a man, to hide his sexual orientation
SYN: maricón, chati,

bujarrón, buja, bujarra, cherna, yegua, pargo, pájaro
✐ *Ese es bugarrón, ¿no lo sabías?*

bujarrón or **bujarra** or **buja**: see *bugarrón*

buldózer: a bulldozer

BULDÓZER

buque: a big plate of food
✐ *¿Y este buque por qué? Si yo no como tanto.*

burujón: an accumulation of many things, a lot of something
✐ *Y había un burujón de carros en la calle.*

burumba: 1) a party, to have fun or a great time 2) embroil, entangle
SYN: 1) bonche, guasanga 2) confusión, embrollo
✐ *Se formó tremenda burumba.*

buti: 1) fat, chubby 2) expression for something good or that tastes delicious
SYN: 1) barril
ANT: 1) flaco, rechupao 2) malísimo, estar de truco
✐ *1) Te estás poniendo buti, no comas tanto. 2) ¡Esa carne te quedó buti!*

buzo: dumpster diver, someone looking through trash to find valuables
✐ *Mira un buzo registrando el basurero.*

C

caballito: motorized police
✎ ¡Mira ahí viene un caballito!

caballo: a strong man
SYN: fuerte, fornido
ANT: flojo, blando
✎ ¡Mijo qué fuerte estás, estás hecho un caballo!

cabezón: pig-headed, stubborn
SYN: testarudo
ANT: comprensivo
✎ ¡Qué cabezón eres! ¿No puedes escucharme?

cabilla: penis
SYN: mandao, morronga, pinga, tolete, bicho

cabo: cigarette butt
✎ No tires los cabos en el suelo.

cabrón: 1) a husband whose wife is unfaithful 2) astute person
SYN: 1) tarrúo, cornudo
✎ 1) Tu jefe es un cabrón.

cabuya: a rope, in Eastern Cuba
✎ ¿Tienes cabuya pa' amarrar esto?

CABUYA

caché: style, elegance
✎ Mi mamá se viste con tremendo caché.

cachimba: a pipe for smoking
SYN: pipa
✎ Se me llenó la cachimba de humo.

25

cachimbo: a big pistol or gun
SYN: cafuca
✎ *Ten cuidado con él, tiene tremendo cachimbo.*

cachumbambé: a seesaw

CADECA: stands for *CAsa DE CAmbio*, a currency exchange locations

caerle comején al palo: to have a situation get worse
SYN: caerle comején al piano, caerle carcoma al piano

caerle comején al piano or **caerle carcoma al piano:** to have a situation become more difficult, get worse
SYN: cerrarse el cuadro, cerrarse el dominó, caerle comején al palo
✎ *¡Llegó mi suegra, ahora sí que le cayó comején al piano!*

caerse de la mata: the moment when someone realizes something, perhaps obvious or everyone already knew
SYN: enterarse
✎ *Me caí de la mata cuando supe la noticia de casualidad.*

cafuca: a pistol
SYN: cachimbo
✎ *Llevas cafuca, se nota por encima de la camisa.*

CAFUCA OR CACHIMBO

cagalera: diarrhea
ANT: estreñimiento
✎ *Tengo cagalera desde anoche.*

cagapoquito: weak, feeble, frail
SYN: blandengue, poca cosa
✎ *¡No seas*

cagapoquito!

caguama: an ugly, fat woman

calandracas: a type of worm for fishing
✏ *Dale, que ya tenemos calandracas, dame una caña de pescar.*

caldo: a fart
SYN: peo
✏ *¿Qué comiste? ¡Tremendo caldo que te has tirado!*

caldosa: a traditional soup made with vegetables, fruit, meat and many other things, boiled for hours and served hot
SYN: ajiaco, en la zona central de Cuba
✏ *¿La caldosa ya está lista?*

calenticos: women's hot pant panties, extremely short pants
SYN: blúmers
✏ *Cuando te veo en calentico yo maúllo y aúllo a la luna.*

camaján: a smart-ass
SYN: vivo
ANT: comemierda
✏ *No te hagas el camaján que estás botao.*

cambiar la vaca por la chiva: to make an unfavorable exchange

camello: a two-section public transit vehicle, usually made of a truck
✏ *¡Cogí el camello para ir a La Habana!*

caminar con los codos: stingy
SYN: carne de culo
ANT: espléndido

CANA

cana: jail
SYN: prisión, tanque,

cárcel
✎ ¿Cuánto tiempo estuviste en cana?

canal: 1) a slide 2) the area between the buttocks, butt crack
✎ 2) Ya tú tienes pelos en la canal.

candanga: problems, difficulties
SYN: bateo

¡candela!: 1) fire 2) expression of surprise when something bad happened or is about to happen 3) a problem
SYN: 2) ¡los fósforos! 3) lío, problema
✎ 2) ¡Candela, deje que sepa que robaron en su casa! 3) ¡Dios mío en qué candela nos hemos metido!

candela al jarro: persevere until you reach your goal
✎ ¡Candela al jarro hasta que pierda el fondo, esa mujer será tuya!

canilluo: to have long and skinny legs

canina: to be hungry, to have the desire to eat something
SYN: hambre
✎ ¡Tengo tremenda canina, dame algo de comer!

CANTAR "EL MANISERO"

cantar "El manisero": literally means "to sing The Peanut Vendor song" and means to die
SYN: colgar los tenis, guardar el carro, ponerse la pijama de madera, estirar la pata
ANT: estar vivo
✎ José ya cantó "El manisero".

caña: money
SYN: baro,
guaniquiqui, piticlinis,
pesos, fulas, plata,
pasta, chavito
✎ *¿Tienes caña pá
pagar esto?*

cañona: the use
of force to get
something
✎ *Lo logró a la
cañona.*

cardenales: a type of
kite that is bigger in
size
SYN: chiringa,
cometa, papalote

caretú: a shameless,
sassy person

carmelita: a shade of
brown

carne de culo: a
stingy and greedy
person
SYN: caminar con los
codos

casasola: an
egocentric person

casino: the musical
genre of salsa but
with a Cuban style
✎ *Yo sé bailar casino.*

catao: the switch
that controls the
electricity in a house
or building, from the
English "cut out"
✎ *Quita el catao
para arreglar el
bombillo.*

cayuco: 1) a
stupid, dumb or not
intelligent person 2)
small, narrow boat
SYN: 1) anormal,
bruto, analfaburro,
ñame, ñame
con corbata,
analfacebolleta,
seboruco, berraco,
zocotroco, no tener
dos dedos de frente
2) botecito, canoa
✎ *2) Se fue en su
cayuco río abajo.*

cazuelero:
nosy, intrusive,
meddlesome, a
gossip
SYN: entrometido,

enredador, murmurador
ANT: discreto
✐ *Él es un cazuelero, siempre metiéndose en lo que no son sus asuntos.*

cerrarse el cuadro: to be in a situation that becomes more difficult, your chances are over
SYN: cerrarse el dominó, caerle comején al palo,caerle comején al piano, caerle carcoma al piano

cerrarse el dominó: see *cerrarse el cuadro*

chabacán or **chavacán:** vulgar, crude, coarse
SYN: vulgar, chabacano
✐ *La letra de la canción es muy chabacana. / Muchos cubanos piensan que los jóvenes hablan* chabacanerías.

chalana: a big shoe
✐ *¿Esa chalana te queda bien? Está grandísima.*

chama: a kid
SYN: chamaco, chico, muchacho
✐ *Chama ven acá.*

chamaco: a boy
SYN: muchachito, fiñe, chama

chambelona: a lollipop
SYN: pirulí, chupa-chupa

champola: a juice or shake made by mixing water (or milk), sugar and soursop fruit
✐ *Estaba deliciosa esa champola que me tomé horita.*

30

chance: same as in English
✎ *Dame chance por favor.*

chao pescao (y a la vuelta picadillo): goodbye or see you later
SYN: adiós, nos pillamos
✎ *Chao pescao, mañana nos vemos.*

chapapote: asphalt

chapear: 1) to cut the grass 2) to kill or murder
SYN: 2) afeitar, guisar, ñampiar
✎ *1) Déjame chapear el jardín que el césped está muy alto.*

chati: homosexual
SYN: maricón, bugarrón, bujarrón, buja, bujarra, cherna, yegua, pargo, pájaro

chatino or **tachino:** mashed, fried plantains

SYN: plátano a puñetazos, tostones

chaveta: 1) a rounded knife used by cigar rollers 2) boasting about oneself
✎ *1) El torcedor de cigarros corta con la chaveta. 2) ¡Se te salió la chaveta!*

chavito: money
SYN: peso cubano, baro, guaniquiqui, caña, piticlinis, pesos, fulas, plata, pasta

cherna: an insulting name for homosexual, a fag, a queer
SYN: maricón, chati, bugarrón, bujarrón, buja, bujarra, yegua, pargo, pájaro
✎ *Mi vecino es un cherna.*

chícharos: dried peas

chicharritas: plantain chips
SYN: mariquitas

CHICHARRITAS

chicharrón: 1) fried pork rind 2) a submissive, kiss-up person

chico: an extremely common way to refer to a person of your same age or younger, especially someone you know

CHIRINGA

chiringa: a kite
SYN: papalote, cardenales, cometa

chispaetren (chispa de tren): homemade rum of poor quality, also written as *chispa e' tren*
SYN: ron callejero
✎ *Vamos a tomarnos la botella de chispaetren.*

chivar: to bug, to annoy

chivatear: to snitch on, to denounce
SYN: trompetear
✎ *Caí preso porque me chivatearon.*

chivato or **chivatón:** snitch, informer
SYN: trompeta

chivichana: a wooden homemade sled / go-kart contraption kids in Cuba use to race, also used to transport stuff, like a small wagon
✎ *Le compré una chivichana a mi hijo.*

chivo: 1) a cheat

sheet for a test 2) bicycle
SYN: 2) birula, bicicleta

chochera: deep affection for someone special, like the love that grandparents have for their grandchildren
✎ *Tu abuelo tiene tremenda chochera.*

chola: head
SYN: coco, moropo
✎ *Tiene tremenda chola para los negocios.*

chorro de plomo: a rude person, that nobody likes
SYN: batido de plomo

chotear: mock, make fun of somebody
SYN: dar cuerda, dar chucho

chucho: a whip

chulo: a gigolo, a pimp

SYN: pinguero

chupa-chupa: lollipop
SYN: chambelona, pirulí

chusco: rough, coarse or harsh in texture
✎ *Esos zapatos lucen muy chuscos.*

cicote, **chicote** or **sicote:** foot stench
SYN: peste a pata
✎ *Tienes tremenda peste a cicote.*

coba: 1) good quality clothing 2) talk a lot to convince a person about a topic
✎ *1) ¡Andas con tremenda coba! 2) Tu padre me dio tremenda coba para venderme el carro.*

coco: head
SYN: chola, moropo
✎ *Tiene tremenda cabeza para los negocios.*

COCO

cocotazo: punch the head, a rap on the head
SYN: coscorrón
✐ *Y le metió un cocotazo por portarse mal.*

coger asando maíz: to catch someone off guard
SYN: coger con las manos en la masa

coger botella: see *botella*

coger la confronta: too late to do something

coger lucha: to be troubled by something or someone

coger mangos bajitos: to grab low hanging fruit, do something easy
SYN: beneficiarse

coger pa'l bonche (coger para el bonche): enjoy or have fun at the expense of someone who is going through an embarrassing situation
SYN: coger pa'l trajín

coger pa'l trajín: a person who is poorly treated by everyone else, a whipping boy
SYN: coger pa'l bonche

coger un aire: to expose oneself to the night weather without appropriate clothing, as a result you get an acute and sporadic pain in any part of your body
✐ *Salí sin abrigo anoche y cogí un aire.*

cohete: 1) a prostitute 2) money, currency 3) a gun 4) penis
SYN: 1) guaricandilla, guari, jinetera, bicha, fletera, piruja, petardo 2) baro, caña, piticlinis, pesos, fulas, plata, pasta, chavito, guaniquiqui 3) cafuca, cahimbo 4) cabilla, mandao, morronga, pinga, tolete, bicho, mandao

cojones: balls
SYN: timbales
✎ ¡Lo hago de esta manera por mis cojones!

cojonú: a brave person
SYN: timbalú
✎ ¡Mi tío es tremendo cojonú!

colgar los tenis: to die
SYN: cantar "El manisero," guardar el carro, ponerse la pijama de madera, estirar la pata

colgar el sable: 1) to quit 2) to die
SYN: 1) renunciar, estar quitao, colgar los guantes 2) cantar "El manisero," guardar el carro, ponerse la pijama de madera, estirar la pata
ANT: 1) ser persistente, batallador
✎ 2) Él colgó el sable con la carpintería y ahora tiene otro negocio.

colgar los guantes: to quit
SYN: renunciar, estar quitao, colgar el sable
ANT: ser persistente, batallador
✎ Él colgó los guantes con la carpintería y ahora tiene otro negocio.

comebiblia: see comebola

comebola: 1) a person who says

or does something inconvenient, untimely or inadmissible, by indiscretion, lack of intelligence or consideration 2) used to insult a person or to refer to with contempt
SYN: 1) comebiblia, comecatibía, comefana, comegofio, comemierda, comepinga, comequeque, cometrapo

comecandela: fanatic of the communist system in Cuba
SYN: ñángara, comuñanga, comunistón
ANT: gusano

comegofio: a silly person, goofball
SYN: sanaco
✎ *¡Qué clase de comegofio tú eres!*

comecatibía: see

comebola

comefana: see *comebola*

comemierda: silly, clueless, stupid, a common insult in Cuba
SYN: comebola, guanajo, lerdo, zanaco, cometrapo, comebola, comequeque

comepinga: 1) a person that says something inappropriate 2) ingenius, this word is much stronger and insulting than *comemierda*
SYN: comebola

comequeque: see *comebola*

cometrapo: see *comebola*

comer bola: 1) to waste time 2) do or say something inappropriate or with reckless disregard 3) talk or say silly things

comer tierra: starving, extremely hungry
✐ *¡Esa familia está comiendo tierra!*

comerse un cable: to have problems, to be in a bad economic situation
✐ *¡Esa familia se está comiendo un cable!*

comérsela (¡Se la comió!): to go beyond the limit, beyond the acceptable
SYN: se le fue la mano
✐ *¡Se la comió con esa mala acción que le hizo a su madre!*

comerte por una pata: to take advantage of someone
✐ *¡Ten cuidado! Te comen por una pata en el aereopuerto, que no se te ocurra cambiar tu dinero*

ahí.

compay: a friend; a contraction of the word *compadre* used mostly in the country
SYN: compadre, compañero, amigo

¡completo Camagüey!: an expression said after finishing a task
✐ *¡Arreglé el refrigerador! ¡Completo Camagüey!*

comunistón: a communist
SYN: ñángara, comencandela, comuñanga

comuñanga: a leftist, a communist
SYN: comecandela, comunistón, ñángara

con pinga: a lot of something
SYN: pingal

concuño or **concuña:** from the

word *concuñado*, the spouse of my brother or sister-in-law

conga: dance of African origin

congrí or **congrís:** a traditional Cuban dish of rice and black beans cooked all together, also known as *gallo pinto* in some Central American countries
SYN: arroz congrí, moros y cristianos
✎ *¡El congrí quedó buenísimo!*

consorte: husband and wife, but also said to friends

conuco: a small parcel or piece of soil for crops
SYN: finquita
✎ *Me voy a trabajar para mi conuco.*

¡coño!: expression of surprise or amazement
SYN: ¡Alabao!

crica: pussy
SYN: papaya, bollo

cruzársele los cables: to become crazy, a lunatic
ANT: estar cuerdo
✎ *Se le cruzaron los cables cuando supo que ella murió.*

cuadrar: to be all set, to have everything ready
SYN: amarrar
✎ *Ya el viaje de mañana a la playa lo tengo cuadrao.*

cuartería: a structure or house that has been divided into rooms for the poor people
SYN: solar

cubaneo: celebratory behavior characteristic of cubans

cubo: a bucket
SYN: balde

cucaracha: coward

CUBO

cuchufleta: nosy
✐ *Tu tía es tremenda cuchufleta.*

cucurucho: 1) small cone-shaped cup filled with peanuts or popcorn 2) describes something very small 3) said when a person is very handsome (or pretty) with a great body
✐ *1) Me compré dos cucuruchos de maní. 2) Ella vive en una casita que es un cucurucho.*

cuentametuvida or **cuéntame tu vida:** forms or paperwork that asks the person their life details, resume

cuento chino: a tall tale, a lie

culeco: the butt SYN: fambeco, fondillo, fonil, fotingo, culeco

culero: diaper

CULICAGAO

culicagao: a little boy, young, inmature and unexperienced SYN: fiñe
✐ *Mi sobrino es todavía un culicagao.*

culillo: to be impatient about something, to have an obssesive idea SYN: pejiguera, majomía
✐ *Tiene culillo con irse de compras.*

cúmbila: a close friend
SYN: asere, consorte, ecobio, ambia, compay, monina, nagüe, socio, yunta, pata

curdo or **curda:** drunk
SYN: juma, ajumarse, curdo / curda, nota, jalao, ponerse curda, ponerse como una cuba
ANT: sobrio
✎ *Él está curda por tanto ron que tomó anoche. / Es un curda empedernido y está en tratamiento. / Se puso más curda con ese ron.*

curralo: work
SYN: empleo

cutaras: typical of eastern Cuba sandals or flip flops, usually made by hand
SYN: chancletas, chinelas
✎ *¿Dónde están mis cutaras?*

D

dar cabilla: to fuck
✎ *¿Le diste cabilla a esa chica?*

dar chucho: mocking of a person
SYN: dar cuerda, chotear
✎ *Le dimos tremendo chucho a tu amigo con los zapatos feos esos que se puso.*

dar coba: talk a lot to convince a person about a topic
✎ *Tu padre me dio tremenda coba para venderme el carro.*

dar cuero: to tease, to trick someone

dar la punzada del guajiro: brain freeze
✎ *Cuando me tomé el refresco me dio la punzá del güajiro.*

dar muela: to talk too much

dar pirey: 1) to

fire someone 2) to eliminate

dar tranca: to fight, to beat someone

dar vaselina: to flatter someone with the intention of convincing

darse lija: to be pretentious, arrogant or showy
SYN: ser ostentoso, jactancioso
✐ *Esa muchacha se da tremenda lija porque tiene tremenda casa y un buen carro.*

darse tremendo tanganazo: to hit yourself by accident, bump yourself
SYN: mameyazo

darse un golpe de suegra: to bang your funny bone (in your elbow) really hard
✐ *Me di un golpe de suegra con la esquina de la mesa.*

darse violín: to scratch yourself between your toes

de a Pepe (cojones): to be brusque, violent, to use force

de a viaje: do something quickly and only once

de ampanga: saying to mean to be incredible, to be something else, in a negative sense

de carretilla: by heart, by memory

de fly: 1) a fly ball in baseball 2) when someone enters or arrives unexpectedly
✐ *2) Llegó a mi casa de fly, sin habernos avisado.*

de Pascuas a San Juan: almost never, very seldom
✐ *Yo viajo a Estados Unidos de Pascuas a San Juan.*

de pinga: 1) a very good, excellent person or thing 2) okay, great 3) really bad

de verdura: a colloquial adaptation of the phrase *de verdad* meaning for real, sure, that's right

deja la muela: stop running at the mouth, stop talking so much

descarga: 1) small party, 2) when you have been criticized by another person

descargar: 1) to have occasional sex 2) to argue with or criticize someone

descojonao: tired, beaten, broken

desconchinflado or **desconchunflado:** 1) broken 2) extremely tired
SYN: desmondingao, hecho leña, desguabinao, desguatao, descujeringao, destimbalar, destoletar
ANT: estar entero
✎ 2) *Regresé desconchunflado del trabajo.*

desguabinao: tired, no strength, weakened
SYN: desconchinflado, desmondingao, hecho leña, desguatao, descujeringao

desguabinar: to break
SYN: desconchinflado, desmondingao, hecho leña, desguatao, descujeringao, destimbalar, destoletar
✎ *Se cayó de la mata de mango y se desguabinó todo.*

desguatao: to be

tired or weak
SYN:
desconchinflado,
desmondingao,
hecho leña,
desguabinao,
descujeringao

desmaya: an order
to finish something,
forget about talking,
get back to work
✎ *¡Desmaya ese
tema, chico!*

desmondingao: to
feel tired or weak
SYN:
desconchinflado,
desmondingao,
hecho leña,
desguabinao,
descujeringao

despingar: 1) to
break or smash
something 2) to beat
somebody

destarrar: to have an
accident, to be badly
injured or killed in an
accident

destemplanza: a

mild fever, just high
enough to miss school
or work
✎ *El niño tiene
destemplanza, le di
una aspirina.*

destimbalar or
destimbalarse: to
break or destroy
something
SYN:
desconchinflado,
desmondingao,
hecho leña,
desguabinao,
desguatao,
descujeringao,
destoletar
✎ *Ni el peor enemigo
de la nación hubiera
destimbalado el país
de la manera que lo
han hecho.*

destoletar: 1) to break
2) to get injured in an
accident
SYN:
desconchinflado,
desmondingao,
hecho leña,
desguabinao,
desguatao,
descujeringao,

destimbalar, destarrar

dichavao: yes, of course, you bet
SYN: seguro
✐ *¿Vas a ir a la fiesta? -¡Dichavao que sí!*

doblar el lomo: to work

drinqui: any alcoholic drink
✐ *Dale suave con el drinqui amiga.*

DRINQUI

durar como merengue en la puerta de una escuela: gone in a flash, literally "to last as long as candy at a school's door"

durofrío: homemade popsicle
✐ *¡Qué sabroso está este durofrío!*

echar un palo: sexual intercourse, to have sex
SYN: pegar un palo

echar un patín: to run as fast as you can
✐ *Tuvo que echar un patín cuando llegó la policía.*

echar un pestañazo: to take a nap
SYN: echar una surna, tirar un pestañazo

echar un tacón: to dance
✐ *Deberías ir conmigo a echar un tacón.*

ECHAR UNA SURNA

echar una surna: a nap
SYN: echar un

pestañazo

está para galleticas.

ecobio: a close friend
SYN: asere, consorte, ambia, compay, monina, nagüe, socio, cúmbila, yunta, pata

El Caimán: said in reference to the island of Cuba, because of its form resembling a cayman

EL CAIMÁN

el culo del mundo:
Timbuktu, the end of the world
SYN: tumbalamula, en casa del carajo, en casa de la pinga
✐ *Ella vive en el culo del mundo, por las montañas orientales.*

el horno no está para galleticas: things are really bad right now
✐ *Vete para tu casa que aquí el horno no*

el ojo del amo engorda al caballo: saying that expresses how beneficial it is to take care of one's own affairs

el viejo: term of endearment for father

embalao: in a hurry
✐ *Salió embalao por esa puerta.*

EMBARACUTEI

emabracutei or **embaracutey:** to be pregnant
SYN: embarazada, preñada
✐ *La pobre, está embaracutey sin desearlo.*

45

embarajar:
dissimulate

embarcar: 1) to arrive late to an appointment 2) not fulfill a promise

embarque: when things go sideways, come out badly, disappointment caused by not fulfilling your expectations
✎ *¡Tremendo embarque que me diste anoche, te esperé por gusto!*

embollado: foolishly falling in love
✎ *Está embollado con la nueva novia.*

empacho: upset stomach, feeling full after overeating

empajar la pinga: to masturbate
SYN: hacerse una paja, pajearse

emperifollado:

polished, buffed, spruced up
SYN: acicalado
✎ *Salió toda emperifollada con su novio.*

EMPERIFOLLADO

empinar chiringa: 1) to fly a kite 2) to waste time
✎ *1) Él anda empinando chiringa.*

empingao: 1) excellent quality 2) annoyed, mad
SYN: 1) buenísimo, entoletao 2) berreao, encabronao, encojonao, volao
ANT: 1) pésimo, de mala calidad
✎ *1) El carro nuevo que me compré está*

empingao. 2) Estoy
empingao contigo.

emplumar: to save,
collect money
✑ *Cuando emplume*
te mandaré dinero.

en casa de la pinga:
a far away place
SYN: en casa del
carajo, en el culo del
mundo, tumbalamula

en pelota or **en**
pelotas: to be naked
SYN: a la bola
✑ *Entré al cuarto*
y ella estaba en
pelota.

encabronao: angry or
annoyed person
SYN: berreao,
empingao,
encojonao, volao

encangrejarse: to not
be working, broken

encaramarse: to
climb up
SYN: subirse a
✑ *Acaba de*
encaramarse en la

mata de coco.

encojonao: 1)
something or
someone really
good 2) pissed off,
annoyed
SYN: 1) entoletao
2) berreao,
encabronao,
empingao, volao

encuero: 1) naked 2)
broke, with no money

endilgar: 1) to
rename something
2) to pass a problem
onto someone else
SYN: entalingar
✑ *Le endilgué el*
letrero al almendrón y
lo vendí.

enmarihuanao: high,
under the effects of
marjuana

entoletao: very good,
excellent quality
SYN: empingao, estar
en la talla

entrar a machetazos:
a fight with knives or

blades

entre col y col, lechuga: after a bad thing, something good happens
SYN: una de cal y otra de arena

éramos pocos y parió Catana: when you already have a problem, and something else shows up, making things worse
✎ ¡Tuvo hijos gemelos y está sin empleo.¡Éramos pocos y parió Catana!

escachao: 1) financialy broke 2) in problems
SYN: 1) estar arrancao, estar bruja, estar pelao, estar en carne, estar en la fuácata 2) jodido
✎ 1) Si fuese un hombre escachao no lo hubiesen arrestado. 2) Él estaba tan escachao

como líder que había que sacarlo.

escapao: to be in, to stand out, to be the best quality or newest fashion
SYN: estar fuera de liga
✎ ¡Su equipo de música nuevo está escapao!

ese es tu maletín: that's your problem
✎ A mi ni me va ni me viene, ese es tu maletín.

espantar la mula: 1) to leave quickly, run away, to clear off
SYN: zafar, ir en pira, pirarse, tumbar
✎ ¡Espanta la mula que ya esto se acabó!

espantarse tremenda cola: 1) to stand or stay in a long line 2) hear a long speech you have no interest
✎ 1) Además de que hace frio, hay que

espantarse tremenda cola.

especular: to show off your material items
ANT: modesto
✎ *Anda especulando con sus ropas de marca.*

ESPEJUELOS

espejuelos: glasses

espendrúm or **espeldrún:** afro hair

ESPENDRÚM

Esperancejo: a name used for unspecified people, like "Tom, Dick and Harry" in English. Other names used in Spanish are *Fulano, Mengano* and *Sutano*.
SYN: fulano, sutano

esponrrú or **esponrú:** a type of pound cake
✎ *¡Me encanta el esponrrú que hace tu tía!*

estambay: to be waiting for something, from the English of "on standby"
✎ *¡Me tienes en estambay, chica!*

estar a dieta: to not have sex in a long time
SYN: tener tremendo atraso
✎ *Desde que mi esposo viajó hace un mes estoy a dieta.*

estar a toda lecha: to be well off

estar achantao: being quiet, doing nothing, lazy
ANT: está que no para
✎ *Mi cuñado es un*

achantao, no ayuda en nada.

estar al cantío de un gallo: to be close to the current location
ANT: en casa del carajo, en casa de la pinga

estar arrancao: broke, out of money
SYN: estar bruja, estar pelao, estar en carne, escachao, estar en la fuácata
✎ *Lo siento estoy arrancao, no tengo ni un kilo.*

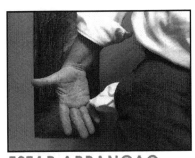

ESTAR ARRANCAO

estar atrás del palo (y pidiendo el último): a clueless person who is behind in the latest news, to be the last person to know something
SYN: estar atrás, despistado, desinformado
ANT: actualizado, informado
✎ *No me sorprende, tu siempre estás atrás del palo. / No se ha enterado de la noticia, está atrás del palo y pidiendo el último.*

estar bruja: out of money, penniless
SYN: estar arrancao, estar pelao, estar en carne, escachao, estar en la fuácata

estar bueno: to be physically attractive, handsome
SYN: bonitillo

estar comiendo de lo que pica el pollo: to act like a fool, not thinking
✎ *¡Hablaste de más, estás comiendo de lo que pica el pollo!*

estar cortao: to have smelly armpits

SYN: grajo, tufado

estar de chúpame y déjame y cabo:
1) great, very good, excellent 2) to be a complex situation
SYN: 2) está de apaga y vámonos
✐ *2) Ese asunto de la herencia está de chúpame y déjame el cabo.*

estar de madre: to behave incorrectly, even hostile, bad
SYN: estar del carajo

estar de pinga: 1) to be annoying, behave incorrectly, to be mad 2) to be good
SYN: 1) estar insoportable

estar de truco: to behave incorrectly, even hostile, horrible
✐ *¡Estás de truco, no hay quien te soporte!*

estar del carajo: to behave incorrectly, even hostile

SYN: estar de madre
✐ *¡Estás del carajo, no hay quien te soporte!*

estar despingado: 1) to be in poor physical shape 2) to be tired and beat up
SYN: muy cansado, herido, accidentado, lastimado
ANT: estar muy bien, en talla

estar embarcao:
to have a problem without a solution, as for example, economic problems
SYN: pasar el Niágara en bicicleta, estar jodido, estrallado

estar en carne (viva):
to be broke
SYN: estar arrancao, estar bruja, estar pelao, escachao, estar en la fuácata
ANT: estar forrao
✐ *¡No tengo ni un peso, estoy en carne!*

estar en la fúacata:

to be broke, penniless SYN: estar arrancao, estar bruja, estar pelao, estar en carne, escachao
✎ ¡Estoy en la fúacata!

estar en talla: 1) to behave exactly as expected in a difficult situation 2) to be perfect, complete, in great condition SYN: 2) entoletao (for an object), empingao
✎ 1) Tu socio está en talla conmigo. 2) El carro que me vendieron está en talla.

estar frito: 1) feeling very tired 2) to be in great difficulties
✎ 1) Estoy frito de tanto trabajar. 2) Salí frito en el examen de inglés.

estar fuera de liga: to stand out, the best SYN: escapao

estar listo pa' la

pelea: literally "to be ready for the fight," to be very fit and well
✎ ¡Ya me siento recuperado del accidente y estoy listo pa' la pelea!

estar mamey: 1) to be good, great, well done 2) when a women is beautiful or sexy 3) when a person conducts him or herself in a pleasant manner ANT: está matao
✎ 1) La fiesta quedó mamey. 2) Esa chica está mamey. 3) Tu amigo se portó mamey conmigo durante la reunión.

estar pelao: penniless, without money SYN: estar arrancao, estar bruja, estar en carne, escachao, estar en la fuácata

estar quitao: to quit SYN: colgar el sable, colgar los guantes, renunciar

estar salao: to have bad luck
✎ ¡Estoy salao, esta semana me han puesto tres multas de tránsito!

estar salío del plato: to be infatuated with, sexually pursuing someone
✎ Ese jovencito está muy salío del plato con la vecina nueva.

estar volao: 1) to be upset 2) drunk
SYN: berreao, encabronao, empingao, encojonao
ANT: calmado
✎ 1) ¡Está volao por lo que le hiciste!
/ ¡Estoy volao del hambre!

este huevo quiere sal: he/she is asking for it, for example when a person demonstrates some kind of intention trying to attract another person to have an affectionate or sexual relationship

esto es un paquete: 1) a problem 2) a lie
✎ 1) Esto de cuidar a dos ancianos enfermos es tremendo paquete.
2) Esto que me acabas de explicar es un paquete, yo sé que me estás mintiendo.

estrallao: a person who is down on their luck, things aren't going well financially

explotar: 1) to explode with anger
SYN: 1) encabronao, salirse por el techo
✎ 1) Explotó por lo que hizo y perdió el trabajo.

explotar como un siquitraque: to explode in anger
✎ Cuando supo de la traición de su mujer, explotó como un siquitraque.

F

fa: powdered detergent to wash the dishes, named for the brand name detergent "Fab"
✐ *Se me acabó el fa.*

fachao: hungry
SYN: pachao
✐ *Me voy a almorzar que estoy fachao.*

fachar: to steal
✐ *Se facharon una antena.*

fajarse: to fight
✐ *¿Te fajaste con él solo porque te ofendió?*

fajazón: a violent fight
SYN: fajarse
✐ *Es posible que no sepas que es un grupo terrorista y empezó esta fajazón.*

fambeco: the butt
SYN: trasero, nalgas, fondillo, fonil, fotingo, culeco
✐ *Van a estar dando patadas por el fambeco a la oposición.*

fanguito: heated, sweetened condensed milk
SYN: dulce de leche

Federico: ugly
ANT: lindo
✐ *Ese muchacho está Federico cantidad, dudo que tenga novia.*

féferes: food
✐ *Voy a comprar los féferes, luego regreso.*

FÉFERES

ferecía or **alferecía:** fear or panic attack
✐ *Fue tanto el disgusto que le dio una ferecía.*

fetecún: a great party
SYN: fiestón
✐ *Anoche metimos tremendo fetecún en mi casa.*

fiana: 1) police patrol car 2) a policeman
✐ *1) ¡Ahí viene la fiana! 2) Ese hombre es un fiana.*

fiesta de perchero: a party where participants are naked, an orgy

fijarse: to cheat on a test
✐ *¿Qué vas a hacer para fijarte en el examen?*

filin: musical movement from the 50's charcterized by romantic songs accompanied with guitars
SYN: bolero

filtro: a smart person
SYN: mechao
ANT: bruto, burro, analfaburro,

analfacebolleta, zocotroco, ser un ñame con corbata
✐ *Pepe es un filtro en Física.*

finalista: a student who studies the day before the exams or when the course is about to end

fiñe: kid, teenager
SYN: culicagao

FIÑE

flechudo: straight hair
ANT: pasas, las pasas, espendrúm
✐ *Tiene el pelo largo y flechudo.*

fletera: a prostitute
SYN: guaricandilla, guari, jinetera, bicha, cohete, piruja,

petardo

florón: person who likes to be the center of attention
🖉 *Parece un florón en medio de la sala.*

¡fo!: bad, unpleasant smell
🖉 *¡Fo, qué peste!*

fondillo: rear-end, heinie
SYN: fambeco, fonil, fotingo, culeco
ANT: desnalgada, planchá
🖉 *¡Tremendo fondoque que tiene esa mujer!*

fongo: a regional name of a small thick-skinned plantain
SYN: plátano burro

fonil: the butt
SYN: fambeco, fondillo, fotingo, culeco

formar arroz con mango or **armar un arroz con mango:**
to create chaos, confusion
🖉 *En la reunión se formó tremendo arroz con mango.*

formar un titingó:
to argue or make trouble, even fighting
🖉 *En el solar se formó tremendo titingó.*

forrajear: make all kinds of efforts to get the necessary articles in short supply
🖉 *Yo forrajeo comida donde sea.*

forro: cheating, especially in games
SYN: mentira, maraña, trampa
🖉 *¡Me metiste un clase de forro ayer en el dominó!*

fotingo: 1) old car, classic or antique 2) the butt
SYN: 2) fambeco, fondillo, fonil, culeco
🖉 *1) Voy a vender el fotingo.*

fotutazo: a horn honk
SYN: pitazo
✐ *¡Qué clase de fotutazo te sonaron!*

frangollo: homemade dessert from fried green plantain ground up and sweetened with syrup
✐ *Estaba muy rico el frangollo que nos comimos.*

frazada (de piso): a rag used to clean the floor
✐ *Necesito comprar una frazada nueva.*

FRÍA

fría: a beer

fricandol: feeling cold, chilly
✐ *Hoy hace tremendo fricandol.*

frigidaire: generic name for a refrigerator
✐ *Apartamento en venta con vista sobre el mar; incluye muebles de la sala, comedor muebles de los dormitorios y frigidaire.*

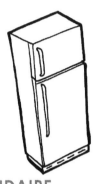

FRIGIDAIRE

friki: in the 80's someone who likes heavy metal music and the fashion that goes with it
✐ *Mi primo es un friki.*

frita (cubana): the Cuban version of a hamburger, no longer made in Cuba. It consisted of a mix of ground beef (sometimes chorizo or pork was added), seasonings, julienne cut potatoes, diced raw onions and ketchup on a Cuban roll. The meat was cooked on a flat top grill.

frozen: a cheap ice cream cone, usually sold for just one peso ✐ *Me acabo de comprar un frozen.*

frutabomba: a papaya fruit in the West part of Cuba

FRUTABOMBA

fuetazo: 1) to give a blow 2) a strong alcoholic drink SYN: 1) aletazo, galúa, piñazo,

viandazo, trompón, avión, tanganazo, mameyazo

fufú (de plátano): mashed, boiled plantain

fula: 1) the CUC (Cuban Convertible Unit) and formerly used to refer to the American dollar 2) a person you can't trust SYN: 1) peso cubano converible, guaniquiqui ✐ *1) ¿Me puedes prestar 5 fulas?*

G

gabinete: a very good house
SYN: gao

gaceñiga: a type of pastry / cake

gallo tapao: phrase used to express uncertainty, when something is not clear or all truth is not known, fishy

galúa: a slap, a hit, a punch, a blow in the face
SYN: aletazo, piñazo, trompón, fuetazo, avión, tanganazo, mameyazo, viandazo

gambao or **gambá:** a bowlegged person

gandinga: 1) dish consisting of cooking the pork entrails 2) extreme patience
✐ *2) Tú tienes tremenda gandinga para estar esperando todo este tiempo.*

gandío: a voracious eater
SYN: glotón, jamaliche
ANT: inapetente, desganado

gangarria: overdone, tacky, or exaggerated jewelry, ornaments or accessories
✐ *Yo me pregunto cómo su cuello aguanta tanta gangarria.*

gao: house
SYN: gabinete
✐ *Voy pa'l gao que es tarde.*

GAO

garapiña: a drink made by fermentating pineapple skin

garrotero: a loan shark

✍ El titular lee "Garroteros mueven la economía popular en Cuba."

gaznatón: a slap on the face
SYN: bofetón, aletazo, puñetazo, galletazo, viandazo
✍ Le metí tremendo gaznatón al tipo ese.

globero: a liar
✍ No la soportan, dicen que es una globera.

globo: a lie

goma: a tire

GOMA

grajo: bad smell in the armpits
SYN: estar cortao, tufado
✍ ¡El tipo tenía tremenda peste a grajo!

guaca or **huaca:** a stash, cache, a hiding place for money
SYN: tener una guanaja echada

guachipupa: a homemade beverage of poor quality, made from sugar and fruit
✍ Me tomé una guachipupa.

GUAGUA

guagua: bus
SYN: rufa
✍ La guagua pasó a su hora.

guaguancó: a musical sub-genre of Cuban rumba

guajiro: the Cuban

61

countryman, a hick
✐ *Le compré frijoles a ese guajiro.*

guanajo: 1) turkey 2) dumb or stupid 3) saved money
SYN: 3) guaca, tener una guanaja echada
✐ *2) Ese niño habla como un guanajo.*

guaniquiqui or **guaniqueque:** money, it could be Cuban pesos, American dollars, or the CUC (Cuban Convertible Unit)
SYN: baro, caña, piticlinis, pesos, fulas, plata, pasta, chavito

guapear: 1) to exert great effort to achieve something 2) to show a provocative attitude, looking for trouble
SYN: 1) guatrapear, pugilateo, ranchear, recorrer las siete estaciones, zapatear, aruñar
✐ *1) Tengo que guapear en mi trabajo por el bien de mi familia. 2) No vengas a guapear a este barrio, vete.*

guapo: a troublemaker, aggressive, bully person who is not scared of fighting
SYN: ambientoso
✐ *¡No te fajes que tú no eres guapo!*

guara: familiarity between people, like a close friendship
SYN: confianza, guaroso

guaracha: 1) a popular dance and music genre 2) fun party

guarandinga: a small bus used for rural transportation
✐ *Se fue en una guarandinga.*

guarapo: refreshing drink made from sugarcane

guararey: a sexy attitude to attract to another person, to flirt

guardar: to imprison
SYN: encarcelar

guardar el carro: to die
SYN: cantar "El manisero," colgar los tenis, ponerse la pijama de madera, estirar la pata
ANT: estar vivo

guarfarina or **gualfarina:** low quality homemade brandy or *aguardiente*
SYN: walfarina

guaricandilla or **guari:** a prostitute, an easy women
SYN: fletera, jinetera, bicha, cohete, piruja, petardo, cohete
✍ *La vecina le dice guaricandilla porque se broncea desnuda en el patio.*

guaroso: a friendly and sociable person who relates to others quickly
✍ *Asere qué guaroso tu eres.*

guasanga: having fun, having a great time
SYN: bonche

guatacón: a kiss-up, fawning person, brown-noser
SYN: tracatán, adulador
✍ *Ese tipo es tremendo guatacón del director.*

guateque: an old term used for a party
✍ *El domingo fuimos a un buen guateque.*

guatrapear: to do everything possible to achieve somthing
SYN: pugilateo, ranchear, recorrer las siete estaciones, zapatear, guapear, aruñar, forrajear

guayaba: 1) the guava fruit 2) a lie

guayabera: linen or cotton shirt which is worn untucked, ideal for use in hot climates, the distinctive design is original from Cuba

guayabito: 1) a small mouse 2) a coward

GUAYO

guayo: kitchen grater, shredder
SYN: rayador
✐ *¿Me prestas un guayo, por favor?*

güije or **jigüe:** a character of the

Cuban mythology, described as a dark-skinned dwarf, matted hair and long, sharp teeth and bulging eyes who lives close to rivers and lakes

GUINEO

guineo: a banana
SYN: platanito
✐ *Esos guineos de la mata de tu patio están riquísimos.*

güiro: 1) a percussion instrument made from a hollow gourd with parallel notches and played by rubbing tines along them 2) the head

guisar: to kill or murder
SYN: afeitar, chapear, ñampiar

gusano: a person who shows his/her unhappiness for the current Cuban government, a dissident
SYN: contrarrevolucionario
✐ *Ese hombre es un gusano.*

hacer el paripé or **hacer un paripé:** see *paripé*

hacer la cruz: 1) do the first business transaction or sale of the day 2) to not take into account someone, to leave them to the side

hacer la media: to accompany someone
SYN: hacer la pala

hacer la pala: to accompany someone, to support
SYN: hacer la media

hacer talco: to destroy someone or something
SYN: desbaratar, despingar
✐ *Lo hicieron talco en la pelea.*

hacer un hijo macho: to cause an emotional harm to

someone
SYN: hacer una
trastada

hacerse de la vista gorda: to ignore what's happening, to play dumb
SYN: hacerse el bizco para verla doble, hacerse el chivo loco, hacerse el chivo con tontera, hacerse el guillao

hacerse el bizco para verla doble: a crafty person who plays dumb to take advantage of a situation, literally translates as "pretending to be cross-eyed to see double"
SYN: hacerse de la vista gorda, hacerse el chivo loco, hacerse el chivo con tontera, hacerse el guillao

hacerse el chivo loco or **hacerse el chivo con tontera:** see *hacerse el guillao*

hacerse el guillao: to play dumb
SYN: hacerse la mosquita muerta, hacerse de la vista gorda, hacerse el bizco para verla doble, hacerse el chivo loco, hacerse el chivo con tontera

hacerse el muerto para ver que entierro le hacen: a person who is lying about a situation, literally translates to "playing dead to see what funeral they give him"
✐ *Esta persona sabe todo esto y más. Le encanta hacerse el muerto para ver qué entierro le hacen.*

hacerse una paja: to masturbate
SYN: empajar la pinga, pajearse

hasta la coronilla: to be stressed, completely up to your ears in something, overwhelmed

hembrona or
hembrota: a
physically attractive
woman, beautiful

hierbero: see *yerbero*

hígado: an
unpleasant, unfriendly
or grouchy person
SYN: bofe, pesao,
inmetible

hueso de la alegría:
the coccyx, tail bone

huevón: a lazy person

I

imperfecto: an
intransigent,
uncompromising and
inflexible person
SYN: hijo de puta,
intransigente
ANT: chévere, mortal
✏ *La profesora
de Física es una
imperfecta.*

**importarle tres
pepinos:** to not care

infumable: see
inmetible

íntimas: feminine
protection pads
✏ *Se me acabaron
las íntimas.*

inmetible: an
ugly person, not
attractive, repulsive

ir en pira: to leave
a place quickly, I'm
leaving
SYN: zafar, espantar
la mula, pirarse,
tumbar
✏ *María, voy en pira*

*porque tengo clase
ahora./ Me voy en
pira para la Florida.*

iriampo or **iria:** food
SYN: jama
✐ *Lo que hace falta
es iria, que tengo
tremenda hambre.*

irse a la americana:
to go Dutch, to pay
50-50
✐ *Vamos a la
americana en
la cuenta del
restaurante.*

jaba: a plastic bag
✐ *Llévate un jaba
para traer el pan.*

jabao or **jabá:** mixed
races of white and
black with very light
skin, pale blonde hair
and black features
such as curly hair
SYN: javao

jabuco: an oversized
bag or *jaba*

jalao: to get drunk
SYN: juma, ajumarse,
curdo / curda (estar
curda), nota, ponerse
curda, ponerse como
una cuba

JAMA

jama: a meal, food
@ *No hay jama en la cocina.*

jamaliche: glutton
SYN: gandío

jamonear: lurking

jamonero: a man who touches or stares at a woman with lust
SYN: mirón, mirahuecos, rescabuchador

janazo: to hit and hurt yourself or by someone

jarana: joking, kidding
SYN: bonche

jarrito: a small metallic mug

jartarse: comes from the word *hartarse* and means to eat food until you feel way too full, stuff yourself

jeba or **jeva:** a boyfriend / girlfriend or with whom you have a romantic relationship
@ *Esa es mi jeva.*

jediondo: stinky

jelengue: a problem, trouble, fight, argument
SYN: problema, lío
@ *¡Tremendo jelengue que se formó!*

jeta: face

jimagua: twins
SYN: mellizos, gemelos

jinetera: a prostitute who only has sex with foreigners
SYN: puta, fletera, guaricandilla, guari, bicha, cohete, piruja, petardo

jiribilla: a restless child

jodienda: problem, dilemma
SYN: problema, lío, pelea

✐ *Me busqué una jodienda con los vecinos.*

jolongo: a cloth or canvas type bag with a rope in the mouth to close or open it

JOLONGO

jugar a los bomberos: to take a bath
✐ *Todavía hoy no he jugado a los bomberos.*

juma: drunk, intoxicated, bombed
SYN: borrachera, emborracharse, ajumarse, curdo / curda (estar curda), nota, jalao, ponerse curda, ponerse como una cuba
✐ *¡Estoy con tremenda juma!*

juntos pero no revueltos: a romantic couple who is not too serious

keta: ketamine drug
✐ *Él consume keta regularmente.*

kilo: the coin equivalent to one cent
SYN: quilo

Visit the SPEAKING LATINO Cuban SPANISH RESOURCE PAGE for more Cuban Spanish and slang Resources!

🖱 http://goo.gl/xhXBPl

L

la antena: the television signal from the US, which is received illegally
✏ *¿Estás cogiendo la antena? ¿Cómo se ve?*

la dolorosa: the bill at a restaurant
✏ *¡Camartero, tráigame la dolorosa!*

LA DOLOROSA

la hora de los mameyes: it is time, it's the moment of truth

la hora del cañonazo: 9:00 pm
✏ *Te espero en el restaurante a la hora del cañonazo.*

la hora en que

72

mataron a Lola: 3:00 pm
✏ *¡Nos vemos a la hora en que mataron a Lola, recuerda!*

la pelona: the death

la vieja: term of endearment for mother

labia: the ability of good oral expression, to be able to convince with the use of words

lagarto: a beer
SYN: láger, fría

láguer: lager beer
SYN: lagarto, fría
✏ *Dame un láguer.*

las pasas: curly hair
SYN: pelo malo, pasas
ANT: flechudo

LAS PASAS

le ronca el mango: see *le zumba el mango*

le zumba el mango: 1) expression of surprise 2) to express bother and frustration, this is the last straw
SYN: maldición, ¡mal rayo me parta!, !me cago en tu madre¡, !me cago en el coño de tu madre!, ¡le zumba el merequetén!, ¡le ronca el mango!, ¡me cago en diez!
ANT: ¡bárbaro!, ¡qué bueno!
✐ *Le zumba el mango que cueste tanto trabajo que alguien te de una mano.*

le zumba el merequetén: see *le zumba el mango*

llanta: shoe

llenarse la cachimba de humo: to be fed up with, angry

llevaitrae (lleva y trae): a gossipy
SYN: bretero, chismoso

¡los fósforos!: 1) expression of surprise over something bad that happened or is about to happen 2) expression of denial or rejection
SYN: 1) ¡candela!
✐ *1) ¡Los fósforos, deja que se entere de que robaron en su finca!*

los viejos: term of endearment for parents

luzbrillante: kerosene
✐ *Llegó la luzbrillante a la bodega.*

M

maceta: a rich person, loaded
✎ *Mi hermano es un maceta.*

machacar las teclas: to play the piano badly
✎ *Ese lo único que hace es machacar las teclas.*

majá: 1) a snake 2) a lazy person who pretends to work
ANT: 2) trabajador
✎ *2) ¡Estoy aquí tirando tremendo majá hasta la hora de almorzar!*

majarete: a sweet made from grated corn, milk and sugar

majasear: to pretend you are working, but really don't
SYN: tirar majá
✎ *Ese hombre está majaseando, no acaba de hacer su trabajo.*

majomía: to be stuck on something, to have an obsessive idea of doing something in specific
SYN: culillo, pejiguera, matraquilla

¡mal rayo te parta!: damn!
SYN: ¡le zumba el mango!, !me cago en tu madre¡, !me cago en el coño de tu madre!, ¡le zumba el merequetén!, ¡le ronca el mango!, ¡me cago en diez!

mala hoja: 1) a man with a short penis, literally a "bad blade" 2) to not be good in bed

malanga: a starchy tropical root or tuber, other names in English are eddoe and taro

malanga y su puesto de viandas: everybody, a lot of people
✎ *Ya lo sabe*

*malanga y su puesto
de viandas.*

malta: wheat soda,
a type of sweet
soft drink, it is a
carbonated malt
beverage, meaning
it is brewed from
barley, hops, and
water much like beer,
but with no alcohol

mameyazo: a blow or
to bump yourself
SYN: darse tremeno
tanganazo, janazo,
batacazo

MAMONCILLO

mamoncillo: a
tropical fruit also
known as throughout
the world as Spanish
lime, genip, guinep,
genipe, ginepa,
quenepa, chenet,
canepa, mamon,
limoncillo in other
countries
SYN: anoncillo in
the central Cuban
provinces

mamoncito: a hicky

**mañana te mando
los aguacates:**
expression used when
someone really won't
follow through with
what was promised,
similar to "don't hold
your breath"
✐ A: *Espero que
mañana me
devuelvas el dinero.
B: Sí, mañana
te mando los
aguacates.*

mandao or **el
mandao:** the penis,
dick
SYN: cabilla,
mandao, morronga,
pinga, tolete, bicho,
cohete

manganzón: a lazy
person, despite being
young and strong

SYN: vago
ANT: trabajador

mango or **mangón:**
attractive person,
good looking
SYN: mangón,
machotote, cuero
✐ *¡Ese artista es un
mango! / El actor
Mario Cimarro es un
mangón.*

MAGO / MANGÓN

marindango:
derogatory word for
a lover

mariquitas: 1)
thin slices of fried
plantain, plantain
chips 2) gays, queers
SYN: chicharritas

maruga: a baby's
rattle

**más quieto que
estate quieto:**
extremely quiet

**más rollo que
película:** something
that doesn't live up to
what was expected
✐ *Tú eres más rollo
que película, nunca
haces lo que dices.*

**más viejo que
Matusalén:** phrase
use to express that
something is really old

mata: a general word
for any plant

MATA

mata de coco: a
woman's boobs
SYN: tetas, melones
✐ *¡Mi primo es un
loco a la mata de
coco!*

mataperrear: the action of spending the day on the street without doing any useful thing

mate: 1) to do everything but have sex 2) to make out

matraquilla: to be obsessed
SYN: majomía, culillo, pejiguera
ANT: desinterés, apatía
✎ *Tiene una clase de matraquilla con esa película.*

matungo: early symptoms of getting sick
SYN: enfermo
✎ *Amanecí matungo.*

mayimbe: a person that holds a high position in the government

me la comí: an expression of excitement, either for good or bad

✎ *Heredé una casa. ¡Me la comí!*

mechao: intelligent, a student who studies hard
SYN: filtro

mecharse: to study hard

medio: the five cent coin

mejunje: a mixture (like a potion)

melones: melons, slang for boobs
SYN: tetas, mata de coco
✎ *¡Ella tiene tremendos melones!*

meta: a policeman
SYN: azulejo, fiana

meter La Habana en Guanabacoa: to try to put something where it does not fit, for example to try to stuff something big into a smaller container

Esos pantalones son una talla más pequeña, no metas La Habana en Guanabacoa.

meter mano: to work
Voy a meterle mano a la construcción de tu casa.

meter una muela: to oversell or speak too much about a topic, to talk to someone for a long time, to convince someone of your opinion

meter una turca: to lie
¡Tremenda turca que le metí a mi jefe para irse temprano!

meterse en camisa de once varas: to get into big trouble
¡Te has metido en camisas de once varas al matar a esa mujer!

meterse en la cajita de dulce guayaba: to die
SYN: cantar "El manisero," colgar los tenis, guardar el carro, ponerse la pijama de madera, estirar la pata
ANT: estar vivo

metimiento: to be in love

michi michi: really bad quality

milordo: a beverage made with brown sugar and water

mima: mommy, mother

mirahuecos: a peeping Tom
SYN: mirón, jamonero, rescabuchador

mocho: 1) an amputee 2) a short piece of something
1) Ese hombre es mocho, perdió la mano derecha hace años.

mojar: to screw, to have sex

mojito: 1) a Cuban cocktail made of white rum, sugar, lime juice, sparkling water, and mint or yerba buena 2) see *mojo*

mojo or **mojito:** any sauce that is made with garlic, olive oil and a citrus juice

mojonera: worthless

molote or **molotera:** a crowd of people

moneda nacional (MN): see *peso cubano*

mono or **mona:** 1) cute, beautiful 2) derogatory name for a police officer
SYN: 2) monada
✎ *Ella es muy mona, todos están enamorados de ella en la escuela.*

monina: a word for friend used in some regions
SYN: asere, consorte, ecobio, ambia, compay, nagüe, socio, cúmbila, yunta, pata

monja: 5 Cuban pesos
✎ *Chico, préstame una monja para pagar el pan.*

morir como Cafunga or **explotar como Cafunga:** a violent death caused by doing something risky

moropo: the head
SYN: coco, chola
✎ *Le dieron por el moropo.*

moros y cristianos: a dish consisting of black beans and white rice all cooked together
SYN: congrí

morronga or **morrongón:** penis, dick

SYN: cabilla, mandao, pinga, tolete, bicho

mortal: something nice, of great quality
✏ *Tu carro nuevo está mortal.*

motivito: a small party
✏ *Le hicieron un motivito por su cumpleaños.*

muela: to talk too much, trying to convince someone of something
✏ *El discurso del presidente fue tremenda muela.*

muengo or **muenga:** a person or animal that is missing an ear

multiplicarse por cero: go away, get out of here
SYN: ¡Vete!
ANT: aparece
✏ *Multiplícate por cero que no quiero verte.*

N

nagüe: a regional word for a friend, dude, pal
SYN: asere, consorte, ecobio, ambia, compay, monina, socio, cúmbila, yunta, pata
✏ *Ese es mi nagüe.*

nananina: negative, a word that means "no," "nothing" or "none"
✏ *Me dijeron que había mucha comida. Nananina, me dejaron pasar hambre.*

ni a jodía: complete rejection, denial

¡ni pinga!: no way, forget it

niche: a black person

niño que no llora, no mama: you need to speak up if you want to be heard
✏ *Pide aumento de*

salario, niño que no llora no mama.

no darle mente: don't think about it
✎ *¡No le des más mente a ese asunto!*

no disparar un chícharo: without putting any effort, to not work, to not anything
SYN: ser un vago
✎ *Me lo dice para seguir viviendo del cuento y ganarse viajecitos sin disparar un chícharo. / No estudia ni dispara un chícharo en su casa.*

no es lo mismo ni se escribe igual: expression to communicate that two things are not related, even though another person is trying to compare them
✎ *No es lo mismo ni se escribe igual que nos vayamos ahora para la playa que la próxima semana, como acordamos.*

no estar en nada: to mind your own business, to be a nice person
✎ *Ella es magnifica, no está en nada.*

no jodas: don't fuck around any more
SYN: no me molestes, no me chives, chivar
✎ *¡No jodas más con ese tema!*

no lo salva ni el médico chino: nothing can save him, literally "not even a Chinese doctor can save him"
✎ *Tiene cáncer, no lo salva ni el médico chino.*

no saber ni papa: to have no idea, to know nothing

no tener dos dedos de frente: a stupid person
✎ *Ese tipo no tiene*

dos dedos de frente,
todo lo hace mal.

no tener madre: an unscrupulous, mean person
✐ *Ese vendedor de seguros no tiene madre.*

no tener pelos en la lengua: a person who speaks his mind

nota: to get drunk
SYN: juma, ajumarse, curdo / curda (estar curda), jalao, ponerse curda, ponerse como una cuba

NOTA

Ñ

ñame: 1) yam 2) a stupid, clumsy, uneducated, unskilled person
SYN: bruto, analfaburro, ñame con corbata, cayuco, analfacebolleta, seboruco, berraco, zocotroco, no tener dos dedos de frente
ANT: 2) inteligente
✐ *1) Me encanta comer ñame con salsa.*

ñame con corbata: a stupid, ignorant or uneducated
SYN: bruto, analfaburro, ñame, cayuco, analfacebolleta, seboruco, berraco, zocotroco, no tener dos dedos de frente
✐ *¿Por qué hay que darle privilegios a este ñame con corbata?*

ñampiar: to kill
SYN: afeitar, chapear,

guisar, pasar por la chágara

ñampiarse: to die SYN: cantar "El manisero," colgar los tenis, guardar el carro, ponerse la pijama de madera, estirar la pata

ñáñara: a skin infection with scabs, a sore, a scratch SYN: yaya
✎ *Estoy lleno de ñáñaras en las piernas.*

ñángara: a communist SYN: comecandela, comuñanga, comunistón
✎ *El jefe es tremendo ñángara.*

ñato: flat-nosed

O - P

obsorbo or **osorbo:** in the *Santería* religion it means all the bad things that are around the person or that can happen to them

ocambo: an old person

pachanga: 1) a party or informal celebration 2) a type of dance performed during carnivals

pachao: see *fachao*

paco: a lot of something

pacotilla: cheap clothing brought from foreign countries to Cuba

paja: to masturbate

pájaro: homosexual, gay SYN: maricón, chati, bugarrón, bujarrón, buja, bujarra, cherna, yegua, pargo

paladar: a small privately owned and operated restaurant but regulated by the government in aspects like the number of seats and the type of food that can be served

palestino: a person that moves to La Habana from the eastern provinces of Cuba

paluchero: someone who talks to mislead, cheat others
SYN: embaucador

pan con timba: bread with guava paste and cheese
SYN: timba

panetela: a type of cake

papalote: a regional word for kite
SYN: chiringa

papaya: pussy in certain parts of Cuba only
SYN: bollo, crica

papayúa: the equivalent to cojonudo, but in reference to a woman:1) to have a large vagina 2) a woman that is bold forcing a difficult situation, brave, with guts 3) lazy
SYN: bollúa

para luego es tarde: It's necessary do it right now

paragüero: someone who drives badly

parece que no moja, pero empapa: someone who does a lot more than is apparent
✐ *Hace muchas cosas a escondidas de sus padres. Ella no moja, pero empapa.*

parejero: a

meddlesome, overfamiliar person
SYN: amistoso, confianzudo
✐ *Ese muchacho me cae bien, es muy parejero.*

pargo: homosexual, gay
SYN: maricón, chati, bugarrón, bujarrón, buja, bujarra, cherna, yegua, pargo, pájaro

paripé: a false appearance or behavior with the intention to achieve a goal, to brag, swank
SYN: hacer el paripé, hacer un paripé

parquear: to park the car

partirle el brazo: to take advantage of a situation

partirle pa' arriba: to face a person or a problem immediately, to attack

pasar como un bólido: to pass by quickly
ANT: pasar como una tortuga
✐ *Pasó como un bólido corriendo frente a mi casa.*

pasar el Niágara en bicileta: to be in a bad financial situation
SYN: estar embarcao

pasar por la chágara: to kill
SYN: afeitar, chapear, guisar, ñampiar

pasarle lo mismo que a Chacumbele (el mismito se mató): to accidentaly harm or kill yourself
✐ *Al anormal este le va a pasar lo mismo que Chacumbele.*

pasas: very curly hair
SYN: pelo malo, las pasas
ANT: flechudo

pasta: 1) money 2)

a sandwich spread usually made from cheese, ham and mayonnaise
SYN: 1) baro, guaniquiqui, caña, piticlinis, pesos, fulas, plata, chavito

pastel: group sex
✐ *Formaron tremendo pastel anoche esas seis personas.*

pastilla: 1) good, nice 2) a pretty girl 3) your special someone, boyfriend or girlfriend

pata: a close friend
SYN: asere, consorte, ecobio, ambia, compay, monina, nagüe, socio, cúmbila, yunta

patatún or **patatús:** a sudden attack, spasm or faint
SYN: soponcio, sirimba, yeyo
✐ *Le dio un patatún con la noticia.*

paticas pa' que te quiero: to run away
✐ *¡Cuando llegó el policía salí paticas pá que te quiero!*

Paticruzado or **Paticruzao:** a brand of Cuban rum

Patilla: a nickname for Fidel Castro

patón: a bad dancer

pegar la gorra: to eat at someone's house without being invited

pegar los tarros or **pegar tarros:** to cheat on one's partner
✐ *Está destrozado, la mujer le pegó los tarros.*

pegar un palo: see *echar un palo*

pajearse: to masturbate
SYN: hacerse una paja, empajar la pinga

pejiguera: a person who is persistent to the point of being annoying
SYN: majomía, culillo, matraquilla
✐ *¡Tiene una pejiguera con el viaje a Varadero!*

pelao sin un kilo: broke, with no money
SYN: estar arrancao, estar bruja, estar estar en carne, escachao, estar en la fuácata

pelo bueno: straight hair
SYN: pelo chino

pelo chino: straight hair
SYN: pelo bueno

pelo malo: curly hair
SYN: pasas, las pasas, pelo pasa

pelo pasa: curly hair

penco: 1) a coward 2) scrawny 3) gay
SYN: 1) pendejo 2) rebejío, rechupao, flacucho

pepa, **pepita** or **perilla:** the clitoris

pepilla or **pepillo:** young woman or man

perder güiro, calabaza y miel: to lose everything
✐ *Lo traicionó y perdió güiro, calabaza y miel.*

perseguidora: police patrol

pescao: 10 Cuban pesos
✐ *¿Me prestas un pescao para pagar la pizza?*

peso cubano: the Cuban peso available for the local population
SYN: peso, peso cubano, peso nacional, moneda nacional (MN)

peso cubano convertible (CUC): the currency used by tourists to buy in stores where U.S. dollars or other currencies were used, it replaces all foreign currencies circulating in stores, restaurants, taxis, hotels. In 2013 the government announced a gradual unification of the *peso cubano* and the CUC
SYN: chavito

pestañazo : to sleep for a short time or take a nap
SYN: echar una surna

petardo: 1) a cheap prostitute 2) an unpleasant, disagreeable person
SYN: 1) fletera, guaricandilla, guari, jinetera, bicha, cohete, piruja 2) pesado

petate: a conversation you have to put up with and don't want to hear, argument
SYN: conversación o discusión larga y aburrida
✎ *Llegó a mi casa y me dio tremendo petate.*

petrolero: see *quemar petróleo*

picú or **picúa**: a tacky, ridiculous person, a person who attempts to be elegant but comes across as ridiculous or tacky

picuencia: tacky or poor taste

pila: in Western Cuba it is the faucet

pimpampun: a cot
✎ *Se vende pimpampun con colchón en muy buen estado.*

pincha: work

pinchar: to work
SYN: laborar
✎ *No quiero pinchar hoy.*

pichicorto: teeny weeny
SYN: mocho

pinga: dick, penis
SYN: morronga, mandao, cabilla
✎ *Lo hago porque me sale de la pinga.*

pingal or **un pingal:** a lot of something
SYN: con pinga, repingal

pinguero: 1) pimp 2) male prostitute, sex worker
SYN: 2) chulo (for man), jinetera (for woman)
✎ *Ese vive de pinguero.*

pingüino: air conditioner
✎ *Este pingüino está buenísimo, me enfría todo el cuarto.*

pingúo: 1) a brave person that acts in his/her best interest, without consideration for others 2) a man with big penis

piñazo: a blow, hit or punch
SYN: aletazo, galúa, trompón, fuetazo, avión, tanganazo, mameyazo, viandazo

piolo: a black person who prefers to have relationships and/or sex with whites
SYN: quemar petróleo

pipa: 1) the belly 2) tank truck

PIPA

piquete: groups of people or friends
✎ *Fuimos a la fiesta en tremendo piquete.*

pirarse: to leave to

89

go away
SYN: tumbar, zumbarse, ir en pira

piruja: a prostitute or easy woman
SYN: fletera, guaricandilla, guari, jinetera, bicha, cohete, petardo
✐ *No salgas con esa piruja.*

pisicorre: small van or station wagon

pitusa: jeans

PITUSA

piticlinis or **piticlín:** money
SYN: baro, guaniquiqui, caña, pesos, fulas, plata, pasta, chavito

90

planchar: to break an agreement, friendship or relationship

plátano a puñetazos: fried, mashed plantains
SYN: chatino, tachino, tostones

plátano burro: see *fongo*

podrida: difficult, annoying and complicated issue or bad news
SYN: barretín, tiñosa

polilla: to be educated, well-read, studious, a voracious reader
✐ *¡Tu prima es una polilla, no para de leer!*

poncharse: 1) a flat tire 2) to flunk a test

ponerle la tapa al pomo: the last straw, the straw that broke the camel's back

ponerse como una cuba: to get drunk
SYN: estar en nota, estar juma, ajumarse, curdo / curda (estar curda), nota, jalao, ponerse curda
ANT: sobrio

ponerse curda: see *curda*

ponerse en tres y dos: to assume a firm position

ponerse la pijama de madera: to die
SYN: cantar "El manisero," colgar los tenis, guardar el carro, estirar la pata

ponérla en China: to ask for something difficult to answer
SYN: ponérsela difícil
✐ *¡Contra, con esa pregunta me la pones en China!*

porsia: abbreviation for "por si acaso" or just in case

portañuela: fly, zipper

PORTAÑUELA

postalita: pretentious or stuck up person
✐ *¡Mira cómo se atreve a decir esto, es un postalita mentiroso que vive del cuento!*

pregonero: a street vendor
✐ *Compré aguacates gracias a los pregoneros.*

prieto: color black

pru: a popular drink made from different plants and roots
✐ *¡Me encanta tomar pru!*

puesto de fritas: small kiosks or carts that prepare fried food to order

91

pugilateo or
pugilatear: efforts
being made to get or
achieve something
SYN: guatrapear,
ranchear, recorrer
las siete estaciones,
zapatear, guapear,
aruñar, forrajear

pulover: a short
sleeve t-shirt

pura: mother or old
lady
SYN: la vieja
✐ *Voy pá casa de la pura.*

puro: father or old
man
SYN: el viejo
✐ *Voy pá casa del puro.*

Q

¿qué bolá?: How's
it going? One of
the most common
greetings said by
Cubans, generally
together with the
word for friend, *asere*
or *acere*
✐ *¿Asere, qué bolá?*

quedarse botao: a
person that does
not understand
something when
explained
SYN: bloqueado
✐ *Me quedé botao.*

**quedarse como el
Gallo de Morón,
sin plumas y
cacareando:** a
phrase used to
express when
someone fails, suffers
a defeat or loses
money, to end up
with nothing

**quedarse para vestir
santos:** to not get
married, a spinster
✐ *Se quedó pa' vestir*

santos, la pobre.

quei or **queik:** Cuban spelling of the English word cake
✐ *¿Trajeron el queik para el cumpleaños?*

quemao: crazy, nuts
SYN: loco, chiflado, loco, quimabo, tener guayabitos en la azotea, tostao
ANT: cuerdo
✐ *Ese tipo está quemao.*

quemar petróleo: to fall in love with a black man or woman
SYN: piolo

quemarse las pestañas: to study hard

querindango: a derogatory word for a lover

quilo: see *kilo*

quimbao or **quimbá:** crazy, nuts
SYN: loco, quemao,
tener guayabitos en la azotea, tostao

quimbar: to have sex
SYN: singar, templar
✐ *¡Qué ganas de quimbar tengo!*

quimbombó: okra

quinqué: a lantern
✐ *Ese quinqué es de buena calidad.*

QUINQUÉ

R

radio bemba or **radiobemba:** a gossipy person

ranchear: a less used word that means to do everything possible to achieve something
SYN: guatrapear, pugilateo, recorrer las siete estaciones, zapatear, guapear, aruñar, forrajear

rascabucheador: a peeping Tom
SYN: mirahueco
✏ *Ese hombre es un rascabucheador.*

RASPA

raspa or **raspita:** crispy rice stuck to the bottom of the pot and can be eaten

✏ *¿Conocen el piropo que dice "si cocinas como caminas, me como hasta la raspita"?*

raspadura: *panela*, a solid piece of sugar obtained from the boiling and evaporation of sugarcane juice

rastra: truck trailer

rayar la pintura: to cheat on a significant other

rebencúo: a stubborn, hard-headed person
✏ *Es un muchacho malcriado y rebencúo.*

rebijío: a puny or very skinny person
SYN: pencho, rechupao

rechupao (rechupado): skinny person
SYN: rebejío, penco

recorrer las siete estaciones: see *forrajear*

relambío (relambido): person who usually assumes a closer or more intimate relationship than is really the case

rencorista: a spiteful person, to hold a grudge
SYN: rencoroso
✐ *Mi error es ser muy rencorista.*

rendir: to beg
✐ *¡No me rindas más!*

repartero: a young person who lives in a ghetto and listens to reggaeton music
✐ *El muchacho ese es un repartero.*

repingal: a huge amount of something, more than a *pingal*
SYN: con pinga

resabioso: cranky, bad tempered

resingar: annoy or pester someone
✐ *Bueno, deja de resingar tanto y te dejamos tranquila.*

retama de guayacol: a mean person, vulgar and poorly educated
✐ *Esa muchacha es retama de guayacol.*

retorcijón: temporary stomach twinges

reventado: to be lucky
SYN: volao

reverbero: spirit lamp, spirit stove

ripiera: a low class person

robarse el show: to grab everyone's attention

ropa vieja: traditional shredded beef stew

rufa: a less used word for a bus

ruinera: horny
✎ ¡Mi jeva está con una ruinera¡

rumba: 1) a type of music and dance 2) a party

saber más que las cucarachas: to be extremely knowledgeable about something
✎ Esa niñita tan pequeña sabe más que las cucarachas.

sacar el hígado: to work extremely hard
✎ Me sacaron el hígado descargando ese camión.

sacar el kilo: to make the most out of something

sacarse la rifa del guanajo: to have the luck (or bad luck) of dealing with something unpleasant or difficult that you didn't expect
SYN: ¡Me la gané!

salación: a misfortune, bad luck
SYN: salar, salarse
✎ ¡Todo me pasa,

tengo una salación!

salfumán or **salfumante:** a household cleaning product made with hydrochloric acid or muriatic acid

salir de la pinga: to say "because I feel like it" or "because I can"
✐ *Lo hago porque me sale de la pinga.*

salpafuera: a disturbance, a problem
SYN: problema
✐ *¡Se formó un salpafuera tremendo!*

salpicón or **salpicona:** a person that likes to flirt

salve: a little help, like lend a little money to tide someone over
✐ *¡Tírame un salve ahí chico!*

sambumbia: a type of beverage made from any kind of fruit
✐ *¡Me tomé una sambumbia que sabía a rayos!*

sancocho: leftover food given to pigs, slop

sandunga: sway, a feminine movement as part of a dance
✐ *Mi negra tiene sandunga.*

sangrón: an annoying person

saoco: rum and coconut water

sapear: to importune, to frustrate, to give bad luck

sapingo or **zapingo:** a person that pretends to be knowledgeable on any material, an ostentatious, undesirable or fake person, imbecile, idiot, moron
✐ *¿Qué se puede esperar de este*

sapingo que se casó con ella?

sapo or **sapa:** an unwelcome and meddling person between a couple

sato: 1) a mutt 2) a promiscuous person SYN: 2) enamoradizo ✐ *2) Ese muchacho es un sato.*

se le está cerrando el cuadro: to have limited or few options

seboruco: dumb, stupid SYN: anormal, bruto, analfaburro, ñame, ñame con corbata, cayuco, analfacebolleta, seboruco, berraco, zocotroco

seguir durmiendo de ese lado: phrase to tell someone to try something new, to react differently than before

seguroso: an informant who works for the MININT, the Cuban State Security Ministry, hated by the Cuban population

ser de ampanga: bad-tempered, controversial, troubled, severe ✐ *Tu suegra es de apanga.*

ser bueno cuando está durmiendo: sarcastic way to refer to a bad person SYN: ser buena persona ✐ *¡Ese primo tuyo es bueno cuando está durmiendo!*

ser como el arroz blanco: to be everywhere at once

ser de ampanga: to be controversial, trouble, to have a strong personality ✐ *Tu suegra es de ampanga.*

ser la candela: an active and naughty person
SYN: ser la pata del diablo

ser la pata del diablo: see *ser la candela*

ser tu maletín: that's your problem
✐ *Tu novia está embarazada por no cuidarse. ¡Ese es tu maletín ahora!*

ser un bicho: smart
SYN: listo
ANT: bruto, analfaburro, ñame, ñame con corbata, cayuco, analfacebolleta, seboruco, berraco, zocotroco, no tener dos dedos de frente
✐ *Vi lo que hiciste ahí, eres un bicho.*

ser un chusma: to be a vulgar person

ser un disco rayado: to be repetitive

ser un echao pa' lante: brave, courageous
SYN: tipo duro

ser un pan: to be good person, a person with a good heart

ser un tipejo: low class, ghetto

ser una mente: to be educated, well-read, studious

sereno: 1) cold air of early evening 2) night watchman
✐ *1) Anoche me dio mucho sereno. 2) Él trabaja como sereno.*

si no es Juana, es su hermana: if it's not one thing, it's another

simbombazo: 1) a hit, a blow 2) to go over badly, to be received poorly
SYN: aletazo, galúa, piñazo, trompón, fuetazo,

avión, tanganazo, mameyazo, viandazo

singao: a son-of-a-bitch
SYN: hijo de puta
ANT: buena gente

singar: to fuck
SYN: templar, quimbar

sirimba: a seizure
SYN: patatún, patatús, soponcio, yeyo
✐ *Le dio una sirimba y la llevaron al hospital.*

socio: a friend
SYN: asere, consorte, ecobio, ambia, compay, monina, nagüe, cúmbila, yunta, pata

socotroco: dumb, stupid
SYN: anormal, bruto, analfaburro, ñame, ñame con corbata, cayuco, analfacebolleta, seboruco, berraco, no tener dos dedos de frente

solar: an old, antique home, generally for rich families, taken over by poor people, converted to slums
SYN: cuartería
✐ *Ella vive en un solar de Centro Habana.*

surnar: to sleep
✐ *No seas tan tonta y ahora déjame ir a surnar.*

T

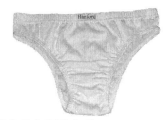

TACASILLO

tacasillo: in central Cuba it is men's underwear
SYN: calzoncillos
✎ *¿Trajiste tacasillos o se te olvidaron de nuevo?*

tachino: see *chatino*

TACHINO / CHATINO

taco: 1) shoes 2) intelligent

tallar: 1) to convince someone to get a certain favor or service 2) to pursue someone, to flirt

tanganazo: a strong blow or hit
SYN: aletazo, galúa, piñazo, trompón, fuetazo, avión, mameyazo, viandazo

tanque: the tank, referring to prison
SYN: cana, cárcel, prisión
✎ *Ya salió del tanque después de 3 meses.*

tapiñar: to cover, to hide something
✎ *No trates de tapiñar algo que es tan obvio.*

tareco: gizmo, thingy

tarro: to cheat in a relationship

tarrúo: the spouse who is cheated on, especially if the relationship continues after finding out
SYN: cabrón, cornudo

tayuyo or **tallullo:** a

regional word for the Cuban tamal
SYN: ayaca, hallaca

temba: a mature person
✏ *Mi padre es un temba.*

templar: to fuck
SYN: quimbar, singar
✏ *Los padres los sorprendieron templando.*

tener 99 papeletas: to have everything in place for something to happen, to have high probabilities

tener abiertas las entendederas: to be open-minded
ANT: bloqueado

tener el cuerpo cortao (cortado): to not be feeling well, generally from fatigue and lack of energy, about to get sick
✏ *No iré a la escuela, tengo el cuerpo cortao.*

tener el moño virao: to be irritable or cranky usually with mood changes and aggressive behavior
✏ *Hoy me levanté con el moño virao y no te voy a pasar ni una.*

tener en el refrigerador: refers to a *santería* ritual of putting an enemy's name written on a piece of paper into the refrigerator, to neutralize their effect on you

tener gandinga: being able to do something that is repulsive, to have the guts to do something
✏ *¡Hay qué tener gandinga para alegar ser inocente despues de ese informe!*

tener guararey: lovesickness

SYN: mal de amores

tener guayabitos en la azotea: to go crazy, literally to have mice in the head
SYN: zafársele un tornillo, zafársele una tuerca, loco, quemao, quimabo, tostao
✎ *Con ese comentario que dices parece que tienes guayabitos en la azotea.*

tener hasta el último pelo: the straw that broke the camel's back, to be fed up with the last thing from a series of negatives

tener la boca cuadrá (cuadrada): a sarcastic expression said when you are not given food or enough food in a place, to not eat
✎ *Se creen que tengo la boca cuadrá que no me*

invitan a comer pollo.

tener los huesos en candela: intense muscular pain, generally from old age
✎ *Mi abuelo tiene los huesos en candela.*

tener tremendo atraso: to not have sex in a long time
SYN: estar a dieta

tener un chino detrás or **tener un chino atrás:** to have bad luck

tener una guanaja echada: hidden stash of money
SYN: guaca, huaca con dinero, guanajo
✎ *Tiene la guanaja enguacá.*

tenerle jiña: to really not like someone, to the point of hating them

tentenpié or **tentempié:** a snack

teque: long and boring conversation that aims to persuade someone to do something

timba: 1) finger food made of two pieces of cheese with a slice of guava paste in the middle 2) a type of music
SYN: 1) pan con timba

timbales: the testicles, balls
SYN: cojones

timbalú: a brave person
SYN: cojonú (for a man), bollúa (for woman)

timbiriche: a small kiosk or business
✐ *Ella trabaja en el timbiriche.*

tiñosa: difficult, annoying and complicated issue
SYN: barretín, podrida

tirar a mondongo: 1) to despise to someone or something 2) to not pay attention to a person or issue
✐ *Me tiró a mondongo y se casó con otra.*

tirar la piedra y esconder la mano: to do something secretly
SYN: hacer cosas a escondidas

tirar majá: to pretend to work, but do nothing
SYN: majasear, majá
✐ *Ese hombre está tirando majá, no acaba de hacer su trabajo.*

tirarse con la guagua andando: to be on the wrong tack

tirarse en el suelo: to feel defeated, give up

tirarse pa'l medio de la calle (tirarse

para el medio de la calle): to behave poorly, completely unacceptably
SYN: botarse pa'l solar

tirarse pa'l solar (tirarse para el solar): see *botarse pa'l solar*

tirisia: 1) yellowish color in newborns 2) untidiness, neglect, laziness
✏ *1) El niño nació con tirisia. 2) Pensar en hacer limpieza me da tirisia.*

titi: a young and pretty woman

titimanía: an old man who likes to have a relationship or sex with much younger women
SYN: viejo verde
✏ *¡Tengo titimanía desde que pasé de los cincuenta años!*

titingó: a confusing, not clear situation,

for example in an aggressive argument
SYN: brete

tocao: 1) something cool, good 2) under the influence of alcohol or drugs
SYN: 2) nota

toletazo: 1) a home run in a baseball game 2) to hit with an object, a blow
SYN: 2) batacazo, trancazo

tolete : dick
SYN: cabilla, mandao, morronga, pinga

tonga: a large amount of something
SYN: tongonal, una tonga, tongón
SYN: pingal

tongón or **tongonal:** see tonga

tortillera: a lesbian
✏ *Ella es tortillera.*

tostao: crazy, nuts

SYN: loco, chiflado, quemao, quimabo, tener guayabitos en la azotea
ANT: cuerdo
✎ *Ese tipo está tostao.*

tostón or **tostones:** fried, smashed green plantain
SYN: tachino in the central zone of Cuba, chatino, plátano a puñetazo

trabajar pa'l inglés (trabajar para el inglés): working so other people benefit from your labor

tracatrán or **tracatán:** a kiss-up, ass kisser, suck-up
SYN: guatacón

trafucar: to confuse
✎ *Realmente lo que quieren es manipular y trafucar la opinión pública.*

tralla: rabble, people with low education

and culture

trancazo: to hit violently
SYN: batacazo, toletazo

trapalero: a dishonest person, a person who cheats or deceives people

trapichante or **trapichero:** a person that works in the black market of illegal goods or things that are difficult to acquire

trapichar: to sell something secretly or illegally

TRESOCHENTICINCO

tresochenticinco: a bottle Havana Club

107

rum, named because the cost is $3.85
SYN: rifle
✐ Compré un tresochenticinco para la fiesta.

trompeta: a whistleblower
SYN: chivato

trompetear: to blow the whistle
SYN: chivatear

trompón: a blow, a hit
SYN: aletazo, galúa, piñazo, trompón, fuetazo, avión, tanganazo, mameyazo, viandazo

tronado: a person is dismissed or fired from his/her job as a punishment

tronar: to fire
✐ ¿Qué pasó con él, lo tronaron?

trusa: a swimsuit

tufado: body odor, stench

SYN: estar cortao, grajo
ANT: oloroso
✐ El taxista está tufado.

TRUSA

tumbalamula: Timbuktu, a far away place
SYN: en casa del carajo, en casa de la pinga, el culo del mundo

tumbando: to go away, to leave
SYN: marcharse, pirarse, zumbarse, zafar, espantar la mula, ir en pira
✐ Me voy tumbando ya.

V

vacilón : to have fun, to enjoy, to do something fun

vejestorio: insulting term for an old person

vejigo or **vejiga:** a kid

VEJIGO

verraquear: to behave like a fool

viandazo: a slap, a blow, a punch
SYN: aletazo, galúa, piñazo, trompón, fuetazo, avión, tanganazo, mameyazo

viejo verde: an old man that likes young woman
SYN: titimanía

volao: 1) to be lucky 2) angry, extremely mad 3) someone who has a high level of skills in a specific discipline 4) hungry
SYN: 1) reventado 2) bravo, berreao, empingao, encabronao, encojonao 3) bárbaro
✎ 2) ¡Estoy volao contigo! 3) ¡Es un volao arreglando computadoras! 4) ¡Estoy volao, qué hambre tengo!

volar el cartucho: when a girl loses her virginity
ANT: ser virgen
✎ A María le volaron el cartucho ayer.

volar el turno: to not bathe today

W - Y

walfarina: see *guarfarina*

yaquis: the Jacks game

YAQUIS

yaya: a skin wound
SYN: ñáñara

yegua: homosexual, gay
SYN: maricón, chati, bugarrón, bujarrón, buja, bujarra, cherna, pargo, pájaro

yeguada: to make a clumsy mistake
✐ *Cometiste una yeguada, ahora tienes que resolver el problema.*

yerbero: a person who grows or sells herbs

SYN: hierbero
✐ *¿Conoces la canción de Celia Cruz que se llama "El yerbero moderno"?*

yeyo: a stroke, faint or seizure
SYN: sirimba, patatún or patatús, soponcio
✐ *¡Ay Dios mío, me va a dar un yeyo!*

yipi: a jeep

YUMA

yuma: 1) U.S.A. 2) a foreigner, usually from the United States
✐ *1) Él vive en la yuma.*

yunta: best friend

110

Z

zafar: 1) unbind, untied 2) to leave, escape from a place or job
SYN: 2) espantar la mula, ir en pira, pirarse, tumbar
✎ 1) Me zafé los cordones de las botas. 2) Me zafé de ese trabajo que no me gustaba.

zambumbia or **sambumbia:** a bad-tasting fruit beverage
✎ ¡Eso sabía a zambumbia!

zamparse: to scarf down food or drink
✎ Me zampé la comida en dos minutos, estaba muy hambriento.

zanaco or **sanaco:** imbecile, asshole, idiot
SYN: tonto
✎ ¡No seas zanaco chico!

zancajear or **zancalejear:** to walk a lot to find something
SYN: tremenda caminata
✎ Tuve que zancalejear La Habana para encontrar esa tela.

zangandongo: something big

zapatear: see *forrajear*

zapingo: see *sapingo*

zocotroco: see *socotroco* dumb, stupid
SYN: anormal, bruto, analfaburro, ñame, ñame con corbata, cayuco, analfacebolleta, seboruco, berraco, no tener dos dedos de frente

zoncear: to fool around

zoquetada:

something foolish,
arrogantly superior

zumbar or **zumbarse:**
1) to overstep the
bounds 2) to leave, to
go away
SYN: 1) mandarse
2) zafar, espantar
la mula, ir en pira,
pirarse, tumbar
✎ 1) *¡Anoche te
zumbaste con mi
hermana!*

zunzún or **zunzuncito:**
the smallest bird in
Cuba

zurdo: a really bad
dancer
✎ *¡Soy zurdo para
bailar!*

THE STORY OF SPEAKING LATINO

Suffering a typical 9-5 existence, Jared's foray into lunch-hour Spanish shook up his mundane life. He quit his job, stopped by briefly to school, and then left the US…for 14 years. Early stumblings in real-world Spanish taught him that a cola isn't just a soft drink, **bicho** doesn't always mean a bug, and **boludo** may be heartfelt or middle-finger felt. Twelve countries, three startups, two bestsellers and a Puerto Rican wife later, he's still confounded by how many Spanish words exist for "panties."

Their personal experiences highlight common confusions of every-day Spanish. With the views of a native Spanish speaker and a gringo who picked it up as an adult, they constantly find entertaining and controversial lessons on how to communicate in Spanish. The Speaking Latino books and website are a consequence of Jared's bumblings in Spanish, crossed communications

Jared

Diana

with Diana, repeated bouts with culture shock, and confusions over the correct words for **popcorn**, gasoline, **pen**, bus, underwear, traffic jam and **drinking straw**. One of the strangest things for him to accept while learning Spanish was why he spent years in classes, and yet a large portion of the words he learned didn't do a bit of good in the real world. It still amazes him that depending on where you are (*chiringa, barrilete, papalote, papagayo, pandorga, chichigua, cometa* or *volantín*) all mean the same thing: **kite**.

Diana, a native Spanish speaker, and Jared, a fluent Spanish speaker who learned the language as an adult, share their research and personal experiences about local Spanish from across the Spanish-speaking world in Speaking Latino. Books and eBooks that collect and translate thousands of Spanish slang words and phrases, articles on Spanish used in specific countries, Spanish learning tips and a searchable Spanish slang dictionary with tons of local words all move you towards real world Spanish fluency.

Follow their discoveries at **www.speakinglatino.com**.

IT'S EASY TO STAY IN TOUCH WITH

WWW.SPEAKINGLATINO.COM

WWW.YOUTUBE.COM/SPEAKINGLATINO

WWW.PINTEREST.COM/SPEAKINGLATINO

WWW.FACEBOOK.COM/SPEAKINGLATINO

@SPEAKINGLATINO

JARED@SPEAKINGLATINO.COM

115

BOOKS BY SPEAKING LATINO
Visit: http://goo.gl/kJXDNi

ARGENTINA

CHILE

COLOMBIA

CUBA

DOMINICAN REP.

MEXICO 1

MEXICO 2

PERU

PUERTO RICO

PUERTO RICO 2

VENEZUELA 1

VENEZUELA 2

PHOTOS & ILLUSTRATIONS CREDITS

Page 5 Presentation. Public domain image (CC0). http://pixabay.com/es/cuba-la-habana-auto-veterano-200766/

Page 8 Absorbente. ©Speaking Latino.

Page 9 Acojonarse. Public Domain CC0. http://pixabay.com/es/smiley-miedo-ira-enojado-150598/

Page 11 Ají. Public Domain CC0. http://pixabay.com/en/peppers-bell-pepper-sweet-pepper-154377/

Page 11 Ajustador. By Steifer with help of Gytha (Own work) [CC-BY-SA-3.0 via Wikimedia Commons. http://commons.wikimedia.org/wiki/File%3AModern_bra_fullcup.jpg

Page 12 Alfiler de cr:andera. Public Domain CC0. http://pixabay.com/en/baby-pin-people-safety-timothy-23808/

Page 13 Amelcocharse. Public Domain CC0. http://pixabay.com/en/heart-love-luck-man-woman-pair-81202/

Page 17 Bailar la suiza. Public Domain CC0. http://pixabay.com/en/boy-child-jump-rope-activity-30456/

Page 18 Bala. Public domain image License (CC0). http://pixabay.com/en/cigarette-cigar-smoking-lung-cancer-3631/

Page 18 Bañadera. Public Domain CC0. http://pixabay.com/en/bathtub-bath-bathe-shower-155866/

Page 19 Baro. By MyName (Yodel553) Victor Alvarez (Own work) [Public domain], via Wikimedia Commons. http://commons.wikimedia.org/wiki/File%3ACuban_100_Peso_Bill.jpg

Page 19 Bemba. Public Domain CC0. http://pixabay.com/en/eyes-red-black-icon-open-human-35616/

Page 20 Birula. Public Domain CC0. http://pixabay.com/en/red-flat-icon-ride-cartoon-bikes-35987/

Page 21 Blúmer. Dotted panties Uploader: laobc. CC0 PD Dedication. http://openclipart.org/detail/78691/dotted-panties-by-laobc

Page 22 Boniato. Public Domain CC0. http://pixabay.com/en/food-outline-drawing-potato-29988/

Page 23 Botella. Public Domain CC0. http://pixabay.com/es/autoestopista-thumber-hitcher-149876/

Page 24 Buldózer. Public Domain CC0. http://pixabay.com/en/bulldozer-vehicle-construction-site-147278/

Page 25 Cabuya. ©Speaking Latino

Page 26 Cafuca or Cachimbo. CC0 PD Dedication. http://openclipart.org/detail/4399/revolver-by-johnny_automatic

Page 27 Cana. Untitled by neilconway, on Flickr. http://www.flickr.com/photos/neilconway/3812660365/

Page 28 Cantar "El Manisero." Public

117

domain image (CC0). http://pixabay.com/en/dead-outline-drawing-skullcartoon-30192/

Page 30 Chalana. By Mike Gonzalez (TheCoffee) (Own work) [CC-BYSA-3.0 or GFDL, via Wikimedia Commons. http://commons.wikimedia.org/wiki/File%3AHush_Puppy_shoe.jpg

Page 32 Chicharritas. By Scott Ehardt (Own work) [Public domain], via Wikimedia Commons. http://commons.wikimedia.org/wiki/File%3APlantain_chips.jpg

Page 32 Chiringa. Public domain image (CC0). http://pixabay.com/en/green-blue-yellow-outside-orange-48752/

Page 34 Coco. Public domain image (CC0). http://openclipart.org/detail/64/rejons-head-by-rejon

Page 39 Cubo. Public domain image(CC0). http://pixabay.com/en/housewater-pale-car-cartoon-24300/

Page 39 Culicagao. Public Domain CC0. http://pixabay.com/es/personas-ni%C3%B1o-pensamiento-reflexivo-28792/

Page 44 Drinqui. By Andreamicci (Own work) [CC-BY-SA-3.0], via Wikimedia Commons. http://commons.wikimedia.org/wiki/File:Mitch_(cocktail).jpg

Page 44 Echar una surna. Public Domain Image. http://openclipart.org/detail/6801/sleeping-by-addon

Page 45 El Caimán. Public Domain

CC0. http://pixabay.com/en/cuba-country-map-149629/

Page 45 Embaracutei. Public domain CC0. http://pixabay.com/en/awaiting-baby-belly-blue-boy-18886/

Page 46 Emperifollado. Public Domain CC0. http://pixabay.com/es/mujer-vestido-rojo-pasarela-bata-157084/

Page 49 Espejuelos. Public domain image (CC0). http://pixabay.com/en/down-sunglasses-glasses-shades-30373/

Page 49 Espendrúm. Public domain image (CC0). http://pixabay.com/en/man-profile-afro-funky-girl-156554/

Page 50 Estar arrancao. Empty Pockets By danielmoyle on Flickr. http://www.flickr.com/photos/danmoyle/5634567317/

Page 55 Féferes. By Trashy Bags (Own work) [CC-BY-SA-3.0], via Wikimedia Commons. http://commons.wikimedia.org/wiki/File%3ATrashy_Smart_Bag.png

Page 56 Fiñe. Public Domain CC0. http://pixabay.com/en/boy-man-teen-teenager-young-161793/

Page 58 Fría. Public domain image (CC0). http://pixabay.com/en/glass-cup-bottle-cartoonmug-29461/

Page 58 Frigidaire. Public domain image (CC0). http://pixabay.com/en/black-outline-drawing-sketch-white-29345/

Page 59 Frutabomba. PAPAYA By

C.E.I.P. Sambori on Flickr. http://www.flickr.com/photos/45579842@N07/4187619898/

Page 60 Gao. CC0 PD Dedication. http://openclipart.org/detail/28497/house-icon-by-purzen

Page 61 Goma. Public domain image (CC0). http://pixabay.com/en/icon-outline-drawing-marks-car-36705/

Page 61 Guagua. Public domain image (CC0). http://pixabay.com/en/bluevan-car-cartoon-bus-buses-34715/

Page 64 Guayo. By Smial (Own work) [FAL or GFDL 1.2], via Wikimedia Commons. http://commons.wikimedia.org/wiki/File%3AKuechenreibe_IMGP2370_wp.jpg

Page 64 Guineo. Public domain image (CC0). http://pixabay.com/en/monkey-black-green-applefood-25339/

Page 68 Jama. Pollo a la brasa bymorrissey, on Flickr. http://www.flickr.com/photos/morrissey/3210018583/

Page 70 Jolongo. Public domain image (CC0). http://pixabay.com/es/bolsa-el-deporte-azul-157720/

Page 72 La dolorosa. Public domain image (CC0). http://pixabay.com/en/people-man-face-cartoon-about-pay-30148/

Page 72 Las pasas. Coat (BW) By lupzdut via Flickr. http://www.flickr.com/photos/10505805@N00/3118633213/

Page 75 Mamoncillo. Public domain image. http://commons.wikimedia.org/wiki/File:Melicoccus_bijugatus.jpg

Page 76 Mango or mangón. hunk Drawn by: bedpanner. CC0 PD Dedication. http://openclipart.org/detail/168616/hunk-by-bedpanner

Page 76 Mata. Public domain image CC0. http://pixabay.com/en/lavender-flower-spring-pot-soil-1727/

Page 82 Nota. Public domain image CC0. http://pixabay.com/en/stick-symbol-people-man-guy-40577/

Page 89 Pipa. Public domain image CC0. http://pixabay.com/es/cami%C3%B3n-transporte-veh%C3%ADculo-gasolina-146319/

Page 90 Pitusa. By Honeyhuyue (Own work) [Public domain], via Wikimedia Commons. http://commons.wikimedia.org/wiki/File%3AJeans_for_men.jpg

Page 91 Portañuela. Public Domain CC0. http://pixabay.com/en/blue-closeup-view-clothes-close-167057/

Page 93 Quinqué. Public Domain CC0. http://pixabay.com/en/antique-burn-glass-glow-isolated-2124/

Page 95 Raspa ©Speaking Latino

Page 102 Tacasillo. By JoeX attl. wikipedia. (Transferred fromtl. wikipedia by Felipe Aira.) [Publicdomain], from Wikimedia Commons. http://commons.wikimedia.org/wiki/File%3A1puritan.

jpg

For ordering information or special discounts for bulk purchases, please
contact Language Babel, Inc. 1357 Ashford Ave., PMB 384, San Juan,
PR 00907 or by e-mail to *info@speakinglatino.com.*

Printed in the United States of America by Language Babel, Inc.

ISBN-10: 1500573817
ISBN-13: 978-1500573812

Printed in the United States of America by Language Babel, Inc.
Version 1.1

FOR MORE INFORMATION ABOUT THE BOOK VISIT:
www.speakinglatino.com/cuban-spanish

**QUICK GUIDE TO CUBAN SPANISH
END OF PREVIEW**

34390294R00070

Made in the USA
Middletown, DE
19 August 2016